TECHNICALITY OF SPORTS

PRANJAL BORKAR

Contents

ONE

IMPORTANCE OF SPORTS

Sports are important because they can help teach life lessons through sports experiences. Along with encouraging life lessons, sports can also help improve physical and mental health through movement. Sports are additionally important because they help students academically as well as they are just good old fashion fun.

One of the primary reasons why sports are important is because the help teach life lessons.

Many people can testify to how sports experiences have taught them all different types of lessons that have transferred into everyday life.

Sports lessons turn into life lessons very easily. Here are some examples:

Sportsmanship- "A fair and generous behavior or treatment of others". This life lesson can easily be taught during a sports experience and then put into practice during everyday life.

Perseverance- "Persistence in doing something despite difficulty or delay in achieving success". This is a very important life lesson that is taught during sports and in my opinion, is the most important lesson that can be taught. There is one trait that is adherent in almost every successful person and that is perseverance. Far too many times people that haven't learned this extremely important life lesson give up on their dreams or goal too soon because they did not understand the power of perseverance.

Respect- "A feeling of deep admiration for someone or something elicited by their abilities, qualities, or achievements". This is another crucial life lesson that is necessary for success. Sports is a great way to teach this as many times to feel respect for someone you must be a part of a collaboration that requires all people to perform successfully to achieve a goal. Through sports, people will understand that when respect is given people tend to perform better. It also allows people to see the importance of earning respect through appropriate and thoughtful actions.

Honesty- "The quality of being honest". This is a lesson that many times sports can get wrong. Unfortunately, some people will sidestep this lesson to win a competition or game. Although, this is counterproductive because people will soon find out that winning in this manner does not have the same effect and ruins the feeling that comes with winning. Most people realize that winning must be earned and doing so without honesty or integrity is not truly winning. The good news is that regardless of the person's path they will eventually comprehend the lesson in the end and learn the life lesson that playing sports intended.

Cooperation- "The process of working together to the same end". Playing sports teaches this lesson almost like osmosis. When playing team sports, cooperation is present at almost every level of the lesson. Working together toward a common goal is at the essence of all sports philosophy. When people experience this through sports it is easily transferred into their lives and many times with great success.

Leadership- "The action of leading a group of people or an organization". Many times while participating in sports an individual is made to step up and grow into their true potential for the team to succeed. This can inspire a person into a leadership role. People take these experiences of leadership through sports and transfer them into their work or personal life. They see their true potential as a leader and help make their lives as well as other's lives better through good leadership. Also, something that can get misinterpreted is that the opposite of a leader is a follower. This many times can have a negative condition that if you aren't a leader you are insignificant. This is simply not true! If your calling is not as a leader you are then a collaborator. This is just as necessary and important as a leader. Without strong collaborators a team or goal many times will not succeed.

Success requires sacrifice- This is a hard one to teach without sports. Without sports as a guide in learning this lesson many people learn it too late. Athletes find out very quickly that without the sacrifice of hard work and practice that winning does not exist. When people realize how hard people must work to become successful they either step up their game or go a different direction.

One of the primary reasons why sports are important is because the help teach life lessons.

Many people can testify to how sports experiences have taught them all different types of lessons that have transferred into everyday life.

Sports lessons turn into life lessons very easily. Here are some examples:

- *Sportsmanship- "A fair and generous behavior or treatment of others". This life lesson can easily be taught during a sports experience and then put into practice during everyday life.*

- *Perseverance- "Persistence in doing something despite difficulty or delay in achieving success". This is a very important life lesson that is taught during sports and in my opinion, is the most important lesson that can be taught. There is one trait that is adherent in almost every successful person and that is perseverance. Far too many times people that haven't learned this extremely important life lesson give up on their dreams or goal too soon because they did not understand the power of perseverance.*

- *Respect- "A feeling of deep admiration for someone or something elicited by their abilities, qualities, or achievements". This is another crucial life lesson that is necessary for success. Sports is a great way to teach this as many times to feel respect for someone you must be a part of a collaboration that requires all people to perform successfully to achieve a goal. Through sports, people will understand that when respect is given people tend to perform better. It also allows people to see the importance of earning respect through appropriate and thoughtful actions.*

Honesty- "The quality of being honest". This is a lesson that many times sports can get wrong. Unfortunately, some people will sidestep this lesson to win a competition or game. Although, this is counterproductive because people will soon find out that winning in this manner does not have the same effect and ruins the feeling that comes with winning. Most people realize that winning must be earned and doing so without honesty or integrity is not truly winning. The good news is that regardless of the person's path they will eventually comprehend the lesson in the end and learn the life lesson that playing sports intended.

Cooperation- "The process of working together to the same end". Playing sports teaches this lesson almost like osmosis. When playing team sports, cooperation is present at almost every level of the lesson. Working together toward a common goal is at the essence of all sports philosophy. When people experience this through sports it is easily transferred into their lives and many times with great success.

Leadership- "The action of leading a group of people or an organization". Many times while participating in sports an individual is made to step up and grow into their true potential for the team to succeed. This can inspire a person into a leadership role. People take these experiences of leadership through sports and transfer them into their work or personal life. They see their true potential as a leader and help make their lives as well as other's lives better through good leadership. Also, something that can get misinterpreted is that the opposite of a leader is a follower. This many times can have a negative condition that if you aren't a leader you are insignificant. This is simply not true! If your calling is not as a leader you are then a collaborator. This is just as necessary and important as a leader. Without strong collaborators a team or goal many times will not succeed.

Success requires sacrifice- This is a hard one to teach without sports. Without sports as a guide in learning this lesson many people learn it too late. Athletes find out very quickly that without the sacrifice of hard work and practice that winning does not exist. When people realize how hard people must work to become successful they either step up their game or go

a different direction.

Fights Depression- Many times people that are struggling with depression have to rely on antidepressants in order to feel healthy. According to a publication from the University of Bern, "the involvement in sport and physical activity partially encounters the same neurophysiological changes as antidepressants. That is why a large number of meta-analyses showed a positive effect of sport and physical activity on depression."

Minimizes Stress- Physical movement has been long known for its beneficial effects on stress reductions. The Anxiety and Depression Association of America (ADAA) has said, "when stress affects the brain, with its many nerve connections, the rest of the body feels the impact as well. So it stands to reason that if your body feels better, so does your mind. Exercise and other physical activity produce endorphins—chemicals in the brain that act as natural painkillers—and also improve the ability to sleep, which in turn reduces stress." When stress is lowered the body and mind are better prepared to handle what life throws at us and sports is a great way to manage stress.

Mental Toughness- Sports is a great way to help encourage mental Toughness. Mental toughness is a sports psychology term that according to the Journal of Applied Sport Psychology is "having the natural or developed psychological edge that enables you to: generally, cope better than your opponents with the many demands (competition, training, lifestyle) that sport places on a performer." When you are mentally tough, it will help you deal with the stresses that can occur. Sports do apply controlled amounts of stress which if not overdone it can help a person practice dealing with stress which will make it easier to deal with overtime. This can result in mental toughness.

It's Okay To Make Mistakes- One of the best teachers in life is making a mistake. While practicing for a sporting event many mistakes are made. Sports teach us that when someone makes a mistake and that mistake is corrected during practice the athlete has just learned a crucial lesson and it will eventually improve their athletic ability. Sports help us understand that without mistakes the lesson can not be learned. It allows us to understand that mistakes are not as bad as everyone makes them out to be. When we turn our thinking around and understand that mistakes can be a good thing in some situations our mental health can only improve.

Increases Self-Confidence- Participation in sports can increase self-confidence in many ways. When someone is praised for making a good play or positively encouraged to keep going when they make a mistake self-confidence is bound to improve. As well as, when a person is actively playing in a sport they are more likely to be physically fit which can also increase self-confidence. Canadian scientists have found that sixth-grade students boys and girls who were more physically active had considerably higher levels of self-esteem. Whether it is through verbal praise, being physically fit or learning from our mistakes sports can definitely help improve self-confidence.

According to the University of Rochester, "Studies have shown that exercise increases blood flow to the brain and helps the body build more connections between nerves, *leading to increased concentration, enhanced memory, stimulated creativity, and better-developed problem-solving skills. In short, playing sports helps your brain grow and makes it work better."*

A study from the University of Kansas City looking at the performance of students in grades 9 to 12 grade showed more than 97% of student-athletes graduated high school 10% then more than those students who had never participated in sports athletes were also known to have better GPA outcomes than non-athletes.

From the book, Educating the Student Body it states that available evidence suggests that mathematics and reading are the academic topics that are most influenced by physical activity. These topics depend on efficient and effective executive function, which has been linked to physical activity and physical fitness.

Jim Fitzsimmons, Ed.D, director of Campus Recreation and Wellness at the University of Nevada, Reno, says, "What we know is students who exercise regularly—at least 3 times a week—at an intensity of eight times resting (7.9 METS) graduate at higher rates, and earn, on average, a full GPA point higher than their counterparts who do not exercise.

In our modern world, we are always hearing about the latest scores and updates from all major sports teams, whether it is professional, collegiate level, or anything else. For many of us, our lives revolve around the athleticism and competitiveness that makes up sports. Ever since we were children, many of our parents had us involved in different sports or activities that gave us the chance to love them or hate them. But what many people do not notice, is that sports and games play a very important role in our lives.

There are many values that we can obtain from playing, watching, or being involved with sports. The first take-away is the educational value that we receive. When we play games and sports, we grow a sense of discipline on ourselves and our teammates. We make sure that we do all that we can, while our teammates are doing all that they can do as well. They teach us that every minute or second is valuable, and they can truly decide fate. Also, sports and games help us reach goals and overcome challenges in life, because they taught us how to work hard, win, and accept loss when it happens.

Secondly, there are emotional values of sports and games. For many, when there is stress or built up anger, physical activity helps us relieve our emotions and find calming peace. As stated previously, sports teach us how to win and lose. With this, we learn how to control our emotions when handed the end result of a game. More emotional values, are that our sense of team spirit grow. Not only does this help with time on the field or court, but it also helps with when we enter the workforce and must work with others.

Aside from educational and emotional values, we also gain in physical aspects as well. Maintaining our health and physical fitness is very vital to our well-being, so engaging in activities like sports and games truly helps. Along so, playing sports increases our endurance, which leads us into the fact that they also helps us get stronger by helping us lose weight and any unwanted fat, and gain muscle. Studies have also shown that mentally, we get stronger as well, because by exercising and playing sports, we increase our blood flow to all parts of the body, especially the brain, and that helps us with our neuroplasticity.

In all, sports, games, and all physical recreations play a huge role in our everyday lives. From childhood, when our parents put us on teams, to today, where many of us love to play sports and games at all time, we have nothing but positive results and values to take away. Gaining educational, emotional, physical, and mental values are all amazing take-aways from sports, that show to be huge assets in our everyday life. Whether you have a favorite sport or not, go find something you like to play and engage in it!

TWO
MEANING OF SPORTS

No one can say when sports began. Since it is impossible to imagine a time when children did not spontaneously run races or wrestle, it is clear that children have always included sports in their play, but one can only speculate about the emergence of sports as autotelic physical contests for adults. Hunters are depicted in prehistoric art, but it cannot be known whether the hunters pursued their prey in a mood of grim necessity or with the joyful abandon of sportsmen. It is certain, however, from the rich literary and iconographic evidence of all ancient civilizations that hunting soon became an end in itself—at least for royalty and nobility. Archaeological evidence also indicates that ball games were common among ancient peoples as different as the Chinese and the Aztecs. If ball games were contests rather than noncompetitive ritual performances, such as the Japanese football game kemari, then they were sports in the most rigorously defined sense. That it cannot simply beassumed that they were contests is clear from the evidence presented by Greek and Roman antiquity, which indicates that ball games had been for the most part playful pastimes like those recommended for health by the Greek physician Galen in the 2nd century CE.

It is unlikely that the 7th-century Islamic conquest of North Africa radically altered the traditional sports of the region. As long as wars were fought with bow and arrow, archery contests continued to serve as demonstrations of ready prowess. The prophet Muhammad specifically authorized horse races, and geography dictated that men race camels as well as horses. Hunters, too, took their pleasures on horseback.

Among the many games of North Africa was ta kurt om el mahag ("the ball of the pilgrim's mother"), a Berber bat-and-ball contest whose configuration bore an uncanny resemblance to baseball. Koura, more widely played, was similar to football (soccer).

Cultural variation among black Africans was far greater than among the Arab peoples of the northern littoral. Ball games were rare, but wrestling of one kind or another was ubiquitous. Wrestling's forms and functions varied from tribe to tribe. For the Nuba of southern Sudan, ritual bouts, for which men's bodies were elaborately decorated as well as carefully trained, were the primary source of male status and prestige. The Tutsi and Hutu of Rwanda were among the peoples who staged contests between females. Among the various peoples of sub-Saharan Africa, wrestling matches were a way to celebrate or symbolically encourage human fertility and the earth's fecundity. In southern Nigeria, for instance, Igbo tribesmen participated in wrestling matches held every eighth day throughout the three months of the rainy season; hard-fought contests, it was thought, persuaded the gods to grant abundant harvests of corn (maize) and yams. Among the Diola of the Gambia, adolescent boys and girls wrestled (though not against one another) in what was clearly a prenuptial ceremony. Male champions were married to their female counterparts. In other tribes, such as the Yala of Nigeria, the Fon of Benin, and the Njabi of the Congo, boys and girls grappled with each other. Among the Kole, it was the kin of the bride and the bridegroom who wrestled. Stick fights, which seem to have been less closely associated with religious practices, were common among many tribes, including the Zulu and Mpondo of southern Africa.

Enter Caption

Enter Caption

Enter Caption

Enter Caption

Contests for runners and jumpers were to be found across the length and breadth of the continent. During the age of imperialism, explorers and colonizers were often astonished by the prowess of these "primitive" peoples. Nandi runners of Kenya's Rift Valley seemed to run distances effortlessly at a pace that brought European runners to pitiable physical collapse. Tutsi high jumpers of Rwanda and Burundi soared to heights that might have seemed incredible had not the jumpers been photographed in flight by members of Adolf Friedrich zu Mecklenburg's anthropological expedition at the turn of the 20th century.

Long before European conquest introduced modern sports and marginalized native customs, conversion to Islam tended to undercut—if not totally eliminate—the religious function of African sports, but elements of pre-Christian and pre-Islamic magical cults have survived into postcolonial times. Zulu football players rely not only on their coaches and trainers but also on the services of their inyanga ("witch doctor").

Traditional Asian sports

Like the highly evolved civilizations of which they are a part, traditional Asian sports are ancient and various. Competitions were never as simple as they seemed to be. From the Islamic Middle East across the Indian subcontinent to China and Japan, wrestlers—mostly but not exclusively male—embodied and enacted the values of their cultures. The wrestler's strength was always more than a merely personal statement. More often than not, the men who strained and struggled understood themselves to be involved in a religious endeavour. Prayers, incantations, and rituals of purification were for centuries an important aspect of the hand-to-hand combat of Islamic wrestlers. It was not unusual to combine the skills of the wrestler with those of a mystic poet. Indeed, the celebrated 14ᵗʰ-century Persian pahlavan (ritual wrestler) Maḥmūd Khwārezmī was both.

Typical of the place of sport within a religious context was the spectacle of 50 sturdy Turks who wrestled in Istanbul in 1582 to celebrate the circumcision of the son of Murad III. When Indian wrestlers join an akhara (gymnasium), they commit themselves to the quest for a holy life. As devout Hindus, they recite mantras as they do their knee bends and push-ups. In their struggle against "pollution," they strictly control their diet, sexual habits, breathing, and even their urination and defecation.

While the religious aspects of Turkish and Iranian "houses of strength" (where weightlifting and gymnastics were practiced) became much less salient in the course of the 20th century, the elders in charge of Japanese sumo added a number of Shintō elements to the rituals of their sport to underscore their claim that it is a unique expression of Japanese tradition. A somewhat arbitrary distinction can be made between wrestling and the many forms of unarmed hand-to-hand combat categorized as martial arts. The emphasis of the latter is military rather than religious, instrumental rather than expressive. Chinese wushu ("military skill"), which included armed as well as unarmed combat, was highly developed by the 3rd century BCE. Its unarmed techniques were especially prized within Chinese culture and were an important influence on the martial arts of Korea, Japan, and Southeast Asia. Much less well known in the West are varma adi ("hitting the vital spots") and other martial arts traditions of South Asia. In the early modern era, as unarmed combat became obsolete, the emphasis of Asian martial arts tended to shift back toward religion. This shift can often be seen in the language of sports. Japanese kenjutsu ("techniques of the sword") became kendō ("the way of the sword").

Of the armed (as opposed to unarmed) martial arts, archery was among the most important in the lives of Asian warriors from the Arabian to the Korean peninsulas. Notably, the Japanese samurai practiced many forms of archery, the most colourful of which was probably yabusame, whose mounted contestants drew their bows and loosed their arrows while galloping down a straight track some 720 to 885 feet (220 to 270 metres) long. They were required to shoot in quick succession at three small targets—each about 9 square inches (55 square cm) placed on 3-foot- (0.9-metre-) high poles 23 to 36 feet (7 to 11 metres) from the track and spaced at intervals of 235 to 295 feet (71.5 to 90 metres). In yabusame, accuracy was paramount.

In Turkey, where the composite (wood plus horn) bow was an instrument of great power, archers competed for distance. At Istanbul's Okmeydanı ("Arrow Field"), the record was set in 1798 when Selim III's arrow flew more than 2,900 feet (884 metres).

As can be seen in Mughal art of the 16th and 17th centuries, aristocratic Indians—like their counterparts throughout Asia—used their bows and arrows for hunting as well as for archery contests. Mounted hunters demonstrated equestrian as well as toxophilite skills. The Asian aristocrat's passion for horses, which can be traced as far back as Hittite times, if not earlier, led not only to horse races (universal throughout Asia) but also to the development of polo and a host of similar equestrian contests. These equestrian games may in fact be the most distinctive Asian contribution to the repertory of modern sports.

In all probability, polo evolved from a far rougher game played by the nomads of Afghanistan and Central Asia. In the form that survived into the 21st century, Afghan buzkashi is characterized by a dusty melee in which hundreds of mounted tribesmen fought over the headless carcass of a goat. The winner was the hardy rider who managed to grab the animal by the leg and drag it clear of the pack. Since buzkashi was clearly an inappropriate passion for a civilized monarch, polo filled the bill. Persian manuscripts from the 6th century refer to polo played during the reign of Hormuz I (271–273). The game was painted by miniaturists and celebrated by Persian poets such as Ferdowsī (c. 935–c. 1020) and Ḥāfeẓ (1325/26–1389/90). By 627 polo had spread throughout the Indian subcontinent and had reached China, where it became a passion among those wealthy enough to own horses. (All 16 emperors of the Tang dynasty [618–907] were polo players.) As with most sports, the vast majority of polo players were male, but the 12th-century Persian poet Neẓāmī commemorated the skills of Princess Shīrīn. Moreover, if numerous terra-cotta figures can be trusted as evidence, polo was also played by aristocratic Chinese women.

There were also ball games for ordinary men and women. Played with carefully sewn stuffed skins, with animal bladders, or with found objects as simple as gourds, chunks of wood, or rounded stones, ball games are universal. Ball games of all sorts were quite popular among the Chinese. Descriptions of the game cuju, which resembled modern football (soccer), appeared as early as the Eastern Han dynasty (25–220). Games similar to modern badminton were also played in the 1st century. Finally, the Ming dynasty (1368–1644) scroll painting Grove of Violets depicts elegantly attired ladies playing chuiwan, a game similar to modern golf.

While the religious aspects of Turkish and Iranian "houses of strength" (where weightlifting and gymnastics were practiced) became much less salient in the course of the 20th century, the elders in charge of Japanese sumo added a number of Shintō elements to the rituals of their sport to underscore their claim that it is a unique expression of Japanese tradition.

A somewhat arbitrary distinction can be made between wrestling and the many forms of unarmed hand-to-hand combat categorized as martial arts. The emphasis of the latter is military rather than religious, instrumental rather than expressive. Chinese wushu ("military skill"), which included armed as well as unarmed combat, was highly developed by the 3rd century BCE. Its unarmed techniques were especially prized within Chinese culture and were an important influence on the martial arts of Korea, Japan, and Southeast Asia. Much less well known in the West are varma adi ("hitting the vital spots") and other martial arts traditions of South Asia. In the early modern era, as unarmed combat became obsolete, the emphasis of Asian martial arts tended to shift back toward religion. This shift can often be seen in the language of sports. Japanese kenjutsu ("techniques of the sword") became kendō ("the way of the sword").

Of the armed (as opposed to unarmed) martial arts, archery was among the most important in the lives of Asian warriors from the Arabian to the Korean peninsulas. Notably, the Japanese samurai practiced many forms of archery, the most colourful of which was probably yabusame, whose mounted contestants drew their bows and loosed their arrows while galloping down a straight track some 720 to 885 feet (220 to 270 metres) long. They were required to shoot in quick succession at three small targets—each about 9 square inches (55 square cm) placed on 3-foot- (0.9-metre-) high poles 23 to 36 feet (7 to 11 metres) from the track and spaced at intervals of 235 to 295 feet (71.5 to 90 metres). In yabusame, accuracy was paramount.

In Turkey, where the composite (wood plus horn) bow was an instrument of great power, archers competed for distance. At Istanbul's Okmeydanı ("Arrow Field"), the record was set in 1798 when Selim III's arrow flew more than 2,900 feet (884 metres).

As can be seen in Mughal art of the 16th and 17th centuries, aristocratic Indians—like their counterparts throughout Asia—used their bows and arrows for hunting as well as for archery contests. Mounted hunters demonstrated equestrian as well as toxophilite skills. The Asian aristocrat's passion for horses, which can be traced as far back as Hittite times, if not earlier, led not only to horse races (universal throughout Asia) but also to the development of polo and a host of similar equestrian contests. These equestrian games may in fact be the most distinctive Asian contribution to the repertory of modern sports.

In all probability, polo evolved from a far rougher game played by the nomads of Afghanistan and Central Asia. In the form that survived into the 21st century, Afghan buzkashi is characterized by a dusty melee in which hundreds of mounted tribesmen fought over the headless carcass of a goat. The winner was the hardy rider who managed to grab the animal by the leg and drag it clear of the pack. Since buzkashi was clearly an inappropriate passion for a civilized monarch, polo filled the bill. Persian manuscripts from the 6th century refer to polo played during the reign of Hormuz I (271–273).]

The game was painted by miniaturists and celebrated by Persian poets such as Ferdowsī (c. 935–c. 1020) and Ḥāfeẓ (1325/26–1389/90). By 627 polo had spread throughout the Indian subcontinent and had reached China, where it became a passion among those wealthy enough to own horses. (All 16 emperors of the Tang dynasty [618–907] were polo players.) As with most sports, the vast majority of polo players were male, but the 12th-century Persian poet Neẓāmī commemorated the skills of Princess Shīrīn. Moreover, if numerous terra-cotta figures can be trusted as evidence, polo was also played by aristocratic Chinese women.

There were also ball games for ordinary men and women. Played with carefully sewn stuffed skins, with animal bladders, or with found objects as simple as gourds, chunks of wood, or rounded stones, ball games are universal. Ball games of all sorts were quite popular among the Chinese. Descriptions of the game cuju, which resembled modern football (soccer), appeared as early as the Eastern Han dynasty (25–220). Games similar to modern badminton were also played in the 1st century. Finally, the Ming dynasty (1368–1644) scroll painting Grove of Violets depicts elegantly attired ladies playing chuiwan, a game similar to modern golf.

THREE

SPORTS IN ASIA

SPORTS IN ASIA

As a rule, even today, sports aren't played as much as they are outside Asia. Children are generally encouraged to spend their time studying not playing sports.

The Asian Games is played every four years. It was held in Doha, Qatar in 2006. More than 10,000 athletes competed in Olympics-style events as well as in sports such as speed chess, wushu, sepak takraw and soft tennis. The 2010 event in Guangzhou featured 40 sports was dominated by China. The 2014 Asian Games in Inchon, South Korea will be trimmed to 36 sports. The eight non-Olympic ports that are included are baseball, karate, bowling, cricket, kabbadi, sepak takraw, squash and wushu.

There is also an East Asian Games and Southeast Asian Games.

Golf in Asia

Golf is becoming increasingly popular in Asia. It has been popular for some time in Japan and South Korea and attracting new players in China and Southeast Asia. Many elite golf courses are used by foreign tourists than by locals.

Golf was introduced to Asia by the British and the places with the oldest gold traditions tend to be former British colonies. The sport is increasingly seen as an asset for getting head and making contacts in the business world. The 30-tournament Asian Tour, the main pan-Asian circuit, was launched in 2003. The main national golf tournament organizations are the Japan Golf Tour, the China Golf Association, the PGA of Australia, the Korea Golf Association, and the Korean PGA. These groups have discussed merging their tours into a 35-tournament OneAsia "super tour." The Asian Tour has not endorsed the idea, viewing as a threat to its tour.

The Masters and British Open, two of golf's four majors, have made an effort to include more Asia players in part to help expand interest of the sport in Asia. There has been some discussion of relocated the PGA Championship, another major, to Asia but PGA officials said in 2012 that won't happen.

At the 2010 Singapore Open, three blind golfer were allowed to play and join the Asian Tour. The three golfers —— Australia's David Blyth, England's Neil Baxter and Malaysia's Yam Ting Woo, played a three-hole challenge, each paired with a professional who was blindfolded.

Asia has many good women golfers, particularly from South Korea and to a lesser extent Japan. Teams made up of Asian women have defeated international teams.

Top Asia players include Liang Wen Chong, the first Chinese player to win the Order of Merit on the Asian Tour; Jeev Milka Singh, who has won six times on the Asian Tour; and Prayad Marksaeng, the first Thai to qualify for the British Open (in 1999). Singh won twice on the European Tour and was the Asian money king in 2006.

A team of top golfers from Asia squares off against a team of top golfers from Europe in rhe Royal Trophy competition in Bangkok. The tournament was inaugurated in 2006.

Badminton in Asia

Badminton is very popular in Asia. The sport was developed in England in 1875 and named after the state of the Duke of Beaufort but was inspired by paddle games in Asia. Badminton is a sport of deft flicks and dramatic overhead kill shots. A typical doubles match destroys eight to a dozen shuttlecocks.

Shuttlecocks are typically made goose feather and sometimes duck feather, The best ones are with 16 hand-selected goose feather plucked in northern China and punched into a cork base. and held together with string and glue, Sometime a single goose only one or two feathers deemed good enough for a shuttlecock. . They have be able to withstand shots of 150 kph and have a shape that ensure consistent, predicable flights. A tubes of dozens coast $25 in the United States.

At a shuttlecock factory for eh Potsky Racquet and Shuttlecock Co. in Guangzhou the feather are sifted, trimmed from 8 inches siwn to 4 inches, sorted by curvature and inserted into a cork imported from Portugal. Only the thickest and most regular feathers ate used for high grade shuttlecocks. Lowe grade shuttlecocks use thinner, slightly irregular good feathers or duck feathers, which are less durable." The feathers typically sell for 3 cents a piece. The Potsky factory goes through 4.8 million of tem a month.

During the bird flu crisis million of birds that normally provide feathers for shuttlecocks were slaughtered. Shuttlecocks were sold made with inferior feathers. The feathers were finer and the shuttlecocks fell apart. Players around the globe complained. Even top produces could not get the quality feathers they needed.

Sepak Takraw

Sepak Takraw is an interesting sport that you see played all over Southeast Asia. Essentially it is volleyball played without using your hands and arms. It is very exciting to watch a good player leap high into the air, flip around and spike the ball with his foot at 60 miles per hour and then fall on his head and shoulders without hurting himself.

Sepak Takraw is played with a special rattan bag in a badminton court. It is known by different names in different countries: "sipak" in the Philippines, "takraw" in Thailand and "sepak raga" in Malaysia. Sepak Takraw was coined in 1965 at the Southeast Asia Games by combining the Malay word for kick ("speak") and the Thai word for ball surprisingly ""takraw""). Malaysia has lobbied to get "sepak *takraw" accepted as an Olympic sport*

The origin of Sepak Takraw is not known. Malays claim it was invented in Malaysia while Thais claim it was invented in Thailand. The game was reportedly played in royals courts in feudal Malaysia an is associated with the great Malayan hero Hang Tuah. In this version of game participants gathered in a circle and tried to keep the ball from hitting the ground. During the British colonization period, it was played mainly in villages as a s lunchtime pastime by working boys.

Competition sepak takraw is played with three players on a team and has rules similar to volleyball and badminton. Play begins with a served (kicked) and each side is allowed three hits (the same as volleyball) before it is delivered over the net to the other team. The scoring is like badminton. The first team to 15 wins.

Team Sports in Asia

Basketball is very popular in Asia, especially China (See China). Rugby is popular in Japan. Hong Kong hosts a popular rugby sevens tournament and was the site of a Bledisloe Cup game between the All Blacks and Australia. South Korea, the Arabian Gulf and Kazakhstan have fielded international teams. By one estimate there are 90,000 rugby players in Sri Lanka.

Hideki Nomo's spectacular debut with the Dodgers in the American Major Leagues in the 1990s sparked interest in baseball across Asia. Baseball is already very big in Japan, South Korea and Taiwan. The Yankees, Dodgers and the Major Leagues have made a big push in China (See China).

Cricket is big in India, Pakistan, Sri Lanka and Bangladesh. In 2006, ESPN-Star, a Singapore-based sports channel jointly owned by Disney and Rupert Murdoch's News Corp, payed $1.1 billion for the righst to broadcast cricket games through a deal with the International Cricket Council.

Kabbadi

Kabbadi is a traditional, territorial game of tag sometimes regarded as India's national sport. It revolves around players shouting "kabbadi, kabbadi, kabbadi, kabbadi" in one breath while trying to capture opposing players and avoid being captured themselves.

No one knows when or how kabbadi was first invented but is believed that it has been around for centuries and was known under a number of different names — zabar ganana, hututu, chedu-gudu, saunchi-pakki, bhadi-bhadi, do-do-do — depending n where it was played. According to one story the game was inspired by the battle between a tiger trying to catch a person to eat and villagers trying to capture the tiger. The game was first played in an organized form at the Hind Vijay Gymkhana in Barodo in 1923.

Kabbadi is a serious game in South Asia with major competitions between national teams from the countries there. India defeated Sri Lanka 76-13 in the gold medal kabbadi match at the 1999 Asian Games. In India it is recognized as on official sport by the India Olympic Association. There are thousands of kabbadi clubs. The game lends itself to rural India because you don't need any equipment; just a small area to play it.

Rules of Kabbadi

Kabbadi is played on a rectangular 13-x-10 meter field that is divided into two halves by a line drawn across the middle of the field. A team is comprised of seven players, but not all seven players take the field at a given time (the others remain in reserve in "waiting blocks" three meters away from the end lines). A match usually is made up of two 20-minuet halves with five minute interval in between.

Play begins when one player called a "raider" crosses the middle line into the territory of his opponents. While in his opponents territory the player shouts "kabbadi, kabbadi, kabbadi, kabbadi" contin

uously in one breath and tries to capture an opposing player. If the raider touches an opposing player and crosses back into his territory the opposing player is out and the raider's team gets a point. While the raider is in the opponent's territory his opponents are trying to grab and hold him. If the raider pauses and breaths and stops saying kabbadi before he crosses back to his territory he is out and the opponents get a point.

When a player from one team completes his turn as a raider. The other teams gets its turn and sends over a raider. If a raider touches two players and returns safely to his territory all the players he touched are out. If one team manages to get all the opposing players out it gets a bonus of four points and both sides bring back all their players.

It s a very physical game with a lot of wrestling as a raider tries to get back to his territory while his rivals are trying to keep him where he is. A raider just has to get any part of his body over the middle line to be declared safe. If opposing players go out of bounds while trying to hold him or escape they are out. Sometimes it is difficult to tell if a raider has stopped saying kabbadi or not. There are rules that prohibit the opposing players from trying the stop the raider's breathing. If an opposing players does such a thing he is out. The are also rule against players having greasy substances on their body or having fingernails long enough to seriously scratch someone.

Cockfighting in Southeast Asia

Cockfighting is popular in Southeast Asia, especially in the Philippines, Thailand and Bali. In Thailand, competitions are held in sand pit arenas. There is a shrine in Thailand that is filled with statue of roosters. It is dedicated to a 16th century national hero, who was fond of cockfighting.

Melanie Brandy wrote in City Life, Chiang Mai: "Gambling on cockfighting is illegal, but it is one of the few forms of illegal gambling 'overlooked' by authorities. For those interested in seeing a cockfight it can be tricky finding one as venues are not openly advertised...Cockfighting can be an all-day affair. Whisky is drunk, food is eaten and bets are placed. Bookies are easy to spot, with their swiftly moving hands indicating the current odds. Basic knowledge of sports betting is helpful in deciphering how to wager and a little Thai doesn't hurt either. [Source: Melanie Brandy, City Life,

Chiang Mai, October 2003 #]

"Cockfighting is a rural sport and symbolises the rural Thais' appreciation of a good, honest fight. Unlike other Southeast Asian countries, the bout does not last until death and Thai cockfighting does not include spurs, hooks or razorblades. It's a match of true strength and will. Before the matches begin, owners of the sparring birds take extensive time comparing the cocks to determine the fairest fights. Bouts usually last around 15 minutes. If a cock tries to run away or screams in earnest two or three times, the match ends and the winner is determined. Injured cocks are sewn up by onsite surgeons and the next match begins." #

The cockfighting industry was hard hit by the bird flu epidemic in Southeast Asia in the mid 2000s. The sport was banned because the birds were often transported long distance for fights and there worries infected roosters could spread the disease to areas that had not been affected. Some owners treat their injured fighting cocks by sucking the bird's blood. The practice is quite dangerous with bird flu present.

Cockfight in Chiang Rai

Describing a cockfighting event in Chiang Rai, Thailand, Alan Sipress wrote in the Washington Post: "On a recent Sunday, Phapart Thieuviharn, a lifelong cock breeder with intense brown eyes and black hair speckled with gray, pulled up at the cockfighting arena as the dirt parking lot was beginning to fill with pickup trucks. Spectators, mostly men from surrounding provinces, crowded three rows of concrete bleachers below a corrugated metal roof. As the elegant, long-legged roosters began to stalk each other, cries rose from the crowd. Many people barked out wagers. Most pressed closer, in some cases leaning into the ring. [Source: Alan Sipress, Washington Post, April 14, 2005,=]

"As the pair of fighting cocks lunged at each other through the air, spectators surged against the edge of the ring with anticipation. Feathers flew. Blood oozed from wounded eyes and throats. Phapart shifted anxiously on the edge of his seat in the concrete bleachers, clutching the notepad on which he had scribbled his bets. Within moments, when one of the roosters surrendered to its injuries and retreated, hundreds and perhaps thousands of dollars would change hands in the arena, located down a dirt track deep in the rice paddies of northern Thailand. =

"Between the 20-minute rounds, the owners scrubbed the blood off their birds with bare hands, wringing out the rags on the ground. Then, with ordinary thread, they stitched the wounds around their eyes and fed them painkillers. Sometimes, Phapart recounted as he watched the hurried surgery, the injuries are so severe that owners relieve the swelling by sucking out the blood by mouth. =

Raising Fighting Cocks

Alan Sipress wrote in the Washington Post:"Phapart, 47, recalled learning to raise cocks from his father and grandfather. As a boy, he refused to go to the barbershop unless he could take along his favorite rooster. As a teenager, he rose hours before school began to train his cocks and then pitted them against those of his teacher. "When you raise fighting cocks, you see them from the moment you open your eyes in the morning. You can even recognize the way each one coos," Phapart said, wearing a green work shirt and chomping on an ever-present piece of gum. "You have a very *close relationship with your fighting cocks, and the closer you are, the more confident you are about their health. You know their condition." [Source: Alan Sipress, Washington Post, April 14, 2005 *]*

"*When you raise fighting cocks, you see them from the moment you open your eyes in the morning. You can even recognize the way each one coos," Phapart said, wearing a green work shirt and chomping on an ever-present piece of gum. "You have a very close relationship with your fighting cocks, and the closer you are, the more confident you are about their health. You know their condition." ***

"*At a training session "in a farmhouse on the edge of town, two trainers were teaching young cocks to feint and dart by thrusting more seasoned roosters toward them. The men clasped the birds in their bare hands, and their forearms were scarred and swollen from the errant attacks of their pupils. "Train harder," Phapart told them. "They're not really strong enough." At the next stop, a large exercise facility where several roosters had just completed their morning sparring, the trainer was bathing them with a hot, moist towel, scrubbing each feather individually and massaging their muscles. Then, with his fingertips, he fed them a special dish made from the minced flesh of a river fish famed for its brawny nature, mixed with honey and herbs. Fighting cocks represent a lavish investment. A proven winner can sell for as much as $2,500, Phapart said. ***

Cockfighting in the United States

In 2008, Louisiana became the last state to outlaw cockfighting in the United States. In 33 states and the District of Columbia, it is a felony. Virginia toughened its law to *make even attending organized fights a felony. The sport remains legal in the U.S. territories of Puerto Rico, Guam and American Samoa. Cockfighting has a long history in the United States and was a hobby of presidents. George Washington, Thomas Jefferson and Andrew Jackson all enjoyed the sport. Abraham Lincoln got his nickname Honest Abe as a cockfight referee. [Source: Carol Guzy, Washington Post, August 15, 2008 **]*

*Describing a cockfight in Louisiana Carol Guzy wrote in the Washington Post: "Weapons are usually strapped to the legs of each rooster. Some prefer razor-sharp knives, but with gaffs that resemble three-inch ice picks, the fights last longer, Bunch explains. As roosters face off in the circle, hoots and hollers echo throughout the bleachers sprinkled with spectators. Gambling at cockfights has been illegal since the passage of a state Senate bill last year, but the winner of the derby collects a purse from entry fees. ***

*"The spectacle begins, and a flurry of feathers flashes as the birds engage in a furious, fatal dance. Men try to revive the faltering roosters by sucking from their beaks the blood pooled in their lungs. Some wounded birds continue to drag themselves around the pit until, finally, with a mortal stab, the bird dies. The limp body is carried to the trash. "In a way, it's a loss and you feel for the bird itself because you know he did the best he could," Bunch says. ***

See Bird Flu

Soccer in Asia

The Asian Football Confederation (AFC) is the top organizing body for soccer in Asia. There are two distinct regions: East Asia and the Middle East. The AFC has been headquartered in Kuala Lumpur, Malaysia since 1965. Some want it to be moved to a Middle Eastern country such as Qatar or United Arab Emirates. In the early 2000s teams from Oceania such as Australia, New Zealand and Samoa began competing with Asian teams for World Cup berths.

The Asian Champions League — Asia's soccer club championships — is run by the AFC and runs for eight months beginning in March. Asia used to have two club soccer championships: the Asian Club Championship and the Asian Cup Winners Cup. In 2001, the two were merged into an Asian Champions League built along the European model. In 2008, the Asian Champions League was revamped and expanded from 28 to 32 teams from 10 countries and the prize money was increased to $14 million. The total budget for 2009 was $20 million, a big jump from the $4 million in 2008. The prize money for the overall winner in 2009 was $1.5 million, with each group winner taking home $40,000.

Strong Asian teams include Gamba Osaka and the Kashima Reds from Japan, Jeonbuk Hyundai and Hyundai Ulsan from South Korea , big-spending Guangzhou Evergrande from China, Brisbane Roar from Australia,Al Ittihad and Al Hilal from Saudi Arabia, Al Arabi from Qatar, Lekhwiya from Iran, . The champion in 2011 was Qatar's Al Sadd. It beat Jeonbuk Hyundai in the finals in a penalty shootout. Al Ittihad has won the title three times.

World Cup: 4.5 teams from Asia and Oceania (the fifth place team plays a team from another region with the winner earning a World Cup berth). It used to be four teams. Before that it was three teams, plus the winner of a game between the forth best Asian team and the best team from Oceania. In 1999, the entire Asian delegation stormed out of a FIFA meeting to protest the allocations of spots to Asian countries. The Asian delegates wanted five spots (two for the hosts South Korea and Japan and three others) in the 2002 World Cup. FIFA was only will to grant four spots. Asia had 4.5 spots in 2006 (with the fifth place team playing the forth place from North America); 4.5 spots in 2010 and will have 4.5 berths again in 2014.

The qualifying for Asia teams for the 2010 World Cup began with five groups with four teams in each group for a total of 20 teams. The top two teams from each group qualified for the next round. The 10 teams were split into two groups. The top two teams from each of these groups qualified for the World Cup. The third place teams played for the right to play the top teams from Oceania. The winner of that game played the fifth place team from South America, with the winner of that game earning a berth to the World Cup. The qualifications began in October 2008 and ran September 2009.

The Asian Cup is Asia's premier national team competition. Launched in 1956, it is played every four years, usually in the summer, and was last played in 2011. The next one is in Australia. Japan has won it last three out of four times. Iraq won it 2007. South Korea won the first two tournaments. Iran was strong in the late 60s and early 70s. Saudi Arabia dominated in the 1980s and early 1990s. Israel won it 1964 but now competes in Europe.

According to data from the mid 2000s, about 35 million people played socer but adult amd youth female participation was less than 1 percent. At soccer games fans often cheer when their teams has the ball, not just when there is a scoring as is the custom in Europe.

European Soccer Clubs in Asia

Teams like Real Madrid, Manchester United, Barcelona. AC Milan, Juventus are all tried establish a presence in Asia for marketing and profit-making purposes. They have plans to open official stores, themed cafes and set up fan clubs.

There has been some discussion of have English Premeir League teams play regular season games in Asian nation such as Japan, South Korea and Qatar. Premier League games are hugely popular on television in Asia but some worry that too much money is spent on broadcast rights for foreign teams rather than on developing local talent.

Asian Players on European Soccer Teams

In April 2011 AP reported: The bank that sponsors Liverpool wants the club to bring in high-profile Asian players.Standard Chartered executive Gavin Laws outlined his hopes for Liverpool in an interview with The Associated Press on Thursday, saying the bank sees great potential for the club to increase its exposure in the Asian market - where it does most of its business.

"The real power for what Liverpool could do for us, and I think for the English Premier League, is if there was a way *they could nurture foreign players from Asia ... a great Asian player - you see what Park Ji-sung does for Manchester United," Laws, the bank's head of corporate affairs, said at the SoccerEx conference. "The markets in Asia and the Middle East are so nationalistic, they are very proud about their countries. (Matches) become huge events. One appearance from a player, say from Dubai in the Premier League, and you'd have the whole of Dubai watching it."*

"The market is saturated in Europe with so many clubs, how many more merchandise sales are they going to create over the next 10 years?" Laws said. "If the clubs want to do merchandise sales going at an exponential rate you've got to be in China, you've got to be in Korea really getting all the people excited about the game."

In July 2008, AFP reported: Manchester United and other English clubs might have Asians in their squads but you won't find one at Chelsea with chief executive Peter Kenyon ruling out "gimmick" players. Kenyon admits it is a huge market they are keen to tap, he is not interested in hiring players unless they are good enough. And he doesn't think any from Asia are. [Source: AFP, July 28, 2008]

"Our view is that the selection of our players is the ability to be in the Chelsea team," he told AFP. "We are not interested in gimmicks. We are not interested having say an American or an Asian in the team because it represents another revenue stream," he said. Asked if there was an Asian player who was good enough to make the 23-man squad, he replied: "I'm not sure there is one. This isn't anti-Asian, but just the competitive nature of the game. We have 23 players and over last few years have seen the best from many countries and they've not been able to get in our team."

Asian Billionaires Seek English Premier League Teams

In 2007, Ben Sheppard of AFP wrote: "Wealthy Asian businessmen are competing to buy top-flight English football clubs, attracted by the irresistible combination of profit and sporting glory. Thaksin Shinawatra, a billionaire football fanatic who was Thai prime minister until ousted by the military last year, now owns 66 percent of Manchester City and looks close to completing a takeover. And directors at promoted Premiership side Birmingham City have recently agreed to sell 30 percent of their shares to Hong Kong tycoon Carson Yeung, despite reported interest in the club from Indian steel magnate Lakshmi Mittal. [Source: Ben Sheppard, AFP, July 5, 2007]

Industry experts say the trend is likely to continue as English football becomes ever more popular among Asia's vast and increasingly wealthy population -- bringing with it the promise of booming income from TV rights and merchandise."Asian businessmen want to own English football teams because they see Asia, particularly India and China, as the biggest developing market for the Premiership," said Philip Long, football specialist at London accountancy firm PKF."The worldwide love of football is focused at the moment on the English game, and the Asian fan base is well-established and growing fast."

But Long warns that Asian investors are not just signing another business deal when they buy into the Premiership. "Anyone investing in football is making a partly rational, partly romantic decision. That can be a dangerous mix," he said. "It is a different type of investment to any other. "Undoubtedly these businessmen know it is a sector that involves a great deal of publicity, and perhaps that's what *they want. But when you buy a football club, you are taking on many responsibilities."During a losing streak, you must expect to have thousands of people chanting abuse at you."Fans can be very fickle and their financial investment in the club is probably limited to their season ticket, even if they have a huge emotional investment."*

Long has a word of warning both for Asian businessmen craving a Premiership team and for fans who imagine a wealthy Asian buyer may turn their club into world beaters."There is growth in the game now but perhaps it will plateau out soon like Formula One," he said. "And we will see which of these deals actually goes through. Talking about buying a club is one way to attract headlines, but it is a different matter to completing the sale."

One British academic who is advising an overseas consortium on Premiership takeover targets agrees that it is an investment area characterised by high drama and risk. "English soccer is the biggest league in the world with a global audience and hence is attracting international interest," he said, on condition of anonymity."The prestige and status are unique, and new television deals are perceived as offering new value. But the downside is that the current owners are extracting the surplus value when they exit."

Several English clubs are have toured in Asia to boost their support in the region, with Manchester United, Liverpool, Portsmouth and Fulham all playing fixtures. The visitors exemplify the changing face of Premiership boardrooms with Manchester United and Liverpool owned by American tycoons and Portsmouth and Fulham bought up by magnates from Russia and Egypt respectively.

Meanwhile the Asian Football Confederation (AFC) is also running the 16-nation Asian Cup in Indonesia, Malaysia, Thailand and Vietnam.The AFC said it would "obviously" prefer Asian businessmen to invest in the region's own clubs. But, despite such hopes, the pull of the Premiership seems likely to remain strong for Asia's wealthiest.

FOUR

CRICKET

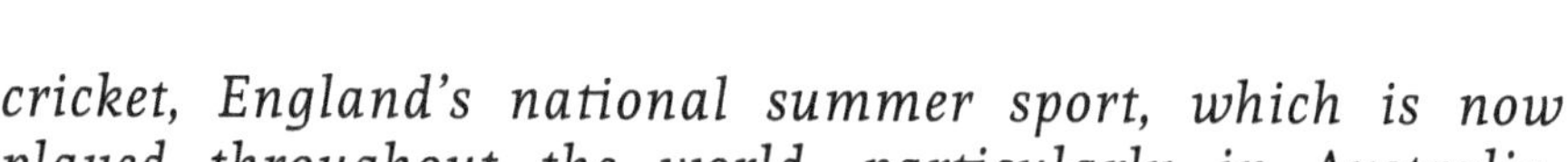

cricket, England's national summer sport, which is now played throughout the world, particularly in Australia, India, Pakistan, the West Indies, and the British Isles.

cricket field

Cricket is played with a bat and ball and involves two competing sides (teams) of 11 players. The field is oval with a rectangular area in the middle, known as the pitch, that is 22 yards (20.12 metres) by 10 feet (3.04 metres) wide. Two sets of three sticks, called wickets, are set in the ground at each end of the pitch. Across the top of each wicket lie horizontal pieces called bails. The sides take turns at batting and bowling (pitching); each turn is called an "innings" (always plural). Sides have one or two innings each, depending on the prearranged duration of the match, the object being to score the most runs. The bowlers, delivering the ball with a straight arm, try to break (hit) the wicket with the ball so that the bails fall. This is one of several ways that the batsman is dismissed, or put out. A bowler delivers six balls at one wicket (thus completing an "over"), then a different player from his side bowls six balls to the opposite wicket. The batting side defends its wicket.

There are two batsman up at a time, and the batsman being bowled to (the striker) tries to hit the ball away from the wicket. A hit may be defensive or offensive. A defensive hit

may protect the wicket but leave the batsmen no time to run to the opposite wicket. In that case the batsmen need not run, and play will resume with another bowl. If the batsman can make an offensive hit, he and the second batsman (the nonstriker) at the other wicket change places. Each time both batsmen can reach the opposite wicket, one run is scored. Providing they have enough time without being caught out and dismissed, the batsmen may continue to cross back and forth between the wickets, earning an additional run for each time both reach the opposite side. There is an outside boundary around the cricket field. A ball hit to or beyond the boundary scores four points if it hits the ground and then reaches the boundary, six points if it reaches the boundary from the air (a fly ball). The team with the highest number of runs wins a match. Should both teams be unable to complete their number of innings before the time allotted, the match is declared a draw. Scores in the hundreds are common in cricket.

Matches in cricket can range from informal weekend afternoon encounters on village greens to top-level international contests spread over five days in Test matches and played by leading professional players in grand stadiums.

Cricket is believed to have begun possibly as early as the 13th century as a game in which country boys bowled at a tree stump or at the hurdle gate into a sheep pen. This gate consisted of two uprights and a crossbar resting on the slotted tops; the crossbar was called a bail and the entire gate a wicket. The fact that the bail could be dislodged when the wicket was struck made this preferable to the stump, which name was later applied to the hurdle uprights. Early manuscripts differ about the size of the wicket, which acquired a third stump in the 1770s, but by 1706 the pitch—the area between the wickets—was 22 yards long.

The ball, once presumably a stone, has remained much the same since the 17th century. Its modern weight of between 5.5 and 5.75 ounces (156 and 163 grams) was established in 1774.

The primitive bat was no doubt a shaped branch of a tree, resembling a modern hockey stick but considerably longer and heavier. The change to a straight bat was made to defend against length bowling, which had evolved with cricketers in Hambledon, a small village in southern England. The bat was shortened in the handle and straightened and broadened in the blade, which led to forward play, driving, and cutting. As bowling technique was not very advanced during this period, batting dominated bowling through the 18th century.

The early years

The earliest reference to an 11-a-side match, played in Sussex for a stake of 50 guineas, dates from 1697. In 1709 Kent met Surrey in the first recorded intercounty match at Dartford, and it is probable that about this time a code of laws (rules) existed for the conduct of the game, although the earliest known version of such rules is dated 1744. Sources suggest that cricket was limited to the southern counties of England during the early 18th century, but its popularity grew and eventually spread to London, notably to the Artillery Ground, Finsbury, which saw a famous match between Kent and All-England in 1744. Heavy betting and disorderly crowds were common at matches.

The aforementioned Hambledon Club, playing in Hampshire on Broadhalfpenny Down, was the predominant cricket force in the second half of the 18th century before the rise of the Marylebone Cricket Club (MCC) in London. Formed from a cricket club that played at White Conduit Fields, the club moved to Lord's Cricket Ground in St. Marylebone borough in 1787 and became the MCC and in the following year published its first revised code of laws. Lord's, which was named after its founder, Thomas Lord, has had three locations over its history. Moving to the current ground in St. John's Wood in 1814, Lord's became the headquarters of world cricket.

In 1836 the first match of North counties versus South counties was played, providing clear evidence of the spread of cricket. In 1846 the All-England XI, founded by William Clarke of Nottingham, began touring the country, and from 1852, when some of the leading professionals (including John Wisden, who later compiled the first of the famous Wisden almanacs on cricketing) seceded to form the United All-England XI, these two teams monopolized the best cricket talent until the rise of county cricket. They supplied the players for the first English touring team overseas in 1859.

The primitive bat was no doubt a shaped branch of a tree, resembling a modern hockey stick but considerably longer and heavier. The change to a straight bat was made to defend against length bowling, which had evolved with cricketers in

Hambledon, a small village in southern England. The bat was shortened in the handle and straightened and broadened in the blade, which led to forward play, driving, and cutting. As bowling technique was not very advanced during this period, batting dominated bowling through the 18th century.

The early years

The earliest reference to an 11-a-side match, played in Sussex for a stake of 50 guineas, dates from 1697. In 1709 Kent met Surrey in the first recorded intercounty match at Dartford, and it is probable that about this time a code of laws (rules) existed for the conduct of the game, although the earliest known version of such rules is dated 1744. Sources suggest that cricket was limited to the southern counties of England during the early 18th century, but its popularity grew and eventually spread to London, notably to the Artillery Ground, Finsbury, which saw a famous match between Kent and All-England in 1744. Heavy betting and disorderly crowds were common at matches.

The aforementioned Hambledon Club, playing in Hampshire on Broadhalfpenny Down, was the predominant cricket force in the second half of the 18th century before the rise of the Marylebone Cricket Club (MCC) in London. Formed from a cricket club that played at White Conduit Fields, the club moved to Lord's Cricket Ground in St. Marylebone borough in 1787 and became the MCC and in the following year published its first revised code of laws. Lord's, which was named after its founder, Thomas Lord, has had three locations over its history. Moving to the current ground in St. John's Wood in 1814, Lord's became the headquarters of world cricket.

In 1836 the first match of North counties versus South counties was played, providing clear evidence of the spread of cricket. In 1846 the All-England XI, founded by William Clarke of Nottingham, began touring the country, and from 1852, when some of the leading professionals (including John Wisden, who later compiled the first of the famous Wisden almanacs on cricketing) seceded to form the United All-England XI, these two teams monopolized the best cricket talent until the rise of county cricket. They supplied the players for the first English touring team overseas in 1859.

motion of the ball. As the grounds improved, however, batsmen grew accustomed to the new bowling style and went on the offensive. Other new bowling styles were also discovered, causing batsmen to adjust their technique further.

W.G. Grace

In the early 20th century so many runs were being scored that debate ensued on reforming the "leg-before-wicket" law, which had been introduced in the 1774 laws to prohibit a batsman from using his body to prevent the ball from hitting his wicket. But the heavy scores were actually due to the performances of several outstanding batsmen, such as W.G. Grace, Sir John Berry Hobbs, and K.S. Ranjitsinhji (later the maharaja of Nawanagar). This was cricket's golden age.

In the 20th century there was a series of attempts to aid the bowler and quicken the tempo of the game. Nevertheless, the game by the mid-20th century was characterized not by overwhelming offense but by defensive play on both sides and by a slow pace. In an attempt to shore up a declining fan base, one-day, or limited-overs, cricket was introduced. One-day cricket had first been played internationally when, *after a Test match was rained out for the first days, on the last scheduled day of play a limited-overs match was held in order to give the fans some game to watch. The response was enthusiastic, and one-day cricket came into being. In this version of cricket the limited number of overs (usually 50 per side) leads to a faster paced though much-altered game. In one-day cricket there are some restrictions on placement of fielders. This led to new batting styles, such as the paddle shot (wherein the ball is hit behind the wicket because there are usually no fielders there) and the lofted shot (where the batsman tries to hit the ball past the fielders and over their heads). Twenty20 (T20), a style of one-day cricket consisting of 20 overs per side, debuted in 2003 and quickly became an international sensation. The first Twenty20 world championship was held in 2007, and one-day cricket, particularly Twenty20, became more popular than Test matches worldwide, although Test cricket retained a large following in England. The pace of Test matches increased dramatically in the late 20th century with the introduction of new bowling strategies.*

Organization of sport and types of competition

County and university cricket

Some of the earliest organized cricket matches were between amateur and professional players. From 1806 (annually from 1819) to 1962, the Gentlemen-versus-Players match pitted the best amateurs against the best professionals. The series was ended in 1962 when the MCC and the counties abandoned the distinction between amateurs and professionals. Other early cricket matches took place between British universities. The Oxford-versus-Cambridge match, for example, has been played mainly at Lord's since 1827 and became a high point of the summer season in London.

University cricket was a kind of nursery for county cricket—i.e., matches between the various counties of England. Although the press acclaimed a "champion county" (Sussex) as early as 1827, qualification rules for county cricket were not laid down until 1873, and it was only in 1890 that the format of the county championship was formalized by the counties themselves. Gloucestershire dominated the 1870s, thanks to W.G. Grace and his brothers E.M. and G.F. Grace. From the 1880s to World War I, Nottinghamshire, Surrey, Yorkshire, Lancashire, Kent, and Middlesex constituted the Big Six that dominated county cricket. After World War I the northern counties, led by Yorkshire and Lancashire, largely professional teams, were the leaders. Surrey, with seven successive championships, dominated in the 1950s and Yorkshire in the 1960s, followed by Kent and Middlesex in the 1970s. The 1980s were dominated by Middlesex, Worcestershire, Essex, and Nottinghamshire. Other counties in first-class county cricket are Leicestershire, Somerset, Hampshire, Durham, Derbyshire, Warwickshire, Sussex, Northamptonshire, and Glamorgan.

After a postwar boom, slow play and lower numbers of runs characterized the 1950s, and this defensive nature of county cricket led to progressively decreased attendance. In the 1960s the MCC and the counties introduced a one-day knockout competition—called the Gillette Cup (1963–1980), the NatWest Bank Trophy (1981–2000), the C&G Trophy (2000–06), and the Friends Provident Trophy (2006–09)—and a separate Sunday afternoon league (the two competitions were merged in 2010 as the Clydesdale Bank 40), which revived public interest, although most counties remained dependent financially on proceeds from football pools and money received from Test matches and broadcasting fees. The immediate registration of overseas players was permitted, and each county, as of the early 1980s, was allowed one such player, who could, however, still play for his national team. The change worked well for the counties, and it also strengthened the national teams for whom those players appeared. In county cricket, bonus points were created to encourage batsmen and bowlers to play less defensively, and from 1988, to help the development of young batsmen and spin bowlers, four-day games increasingly replaced the three-day format. The longer game gives batsmen more time to build an innings and relieves them of the pressure to score runs quickly. Spin bowlers benefit from the longer game because the pitch wears as the game progresses and permits greater spin.

The Cricket Council and the ECB

A reorganization of English cricket took place in 1969, resulting in the end of the MCC's long reign as the controlling body of the game, though the organization still retains responsibility for the laws. With the establishment of the Sports Council (a government agency charged with control of sports in Great Britain) and with the possibility of obtaining government aid for cricket, the MCC was asked to create a governing body for the game along the lines generally accepted by other sports in Great Britain. The Cricket Council, comprising the Test and County Cricket Board (TCCB), the National Cricket Association (NCA), and the MCC, was the result of these efforts. The TCCB, which amalgamated the Advisory County Cricket Committee and the Board of Control of Test Matches at Home, had responsibility for all first-class and minor-counties cricket in England and for overseas tours. The NCA consisted of representatives from clubs, schools, armed services cricket, umpires, and the Women's Cricket Association. In 1997 there was another reorganization, and the TCCB, the NCA, and the Cricket Council were all subsumed under the England and Wales Cricket Boar

International cricket in the early part of the 20th century was dominated by the original members of the Imperial Cricket Conference, England, Australia, and South Africa. Later renamed the International Cricket Conference and then the International Cricket Council, the ICC gradually took over more responsibility for the administration of the game and shifted its power base from west to east. When in 2005 the ICC moved its offices from Lord's in London—home of the MCC, the game's original rulers and still its lawmakers—to Dubai, the shift away from the old ways of governance was complete. The priorities of the game changed too. By the turn of the 21st century, only Australia and England still played Test cricket to full houses. Everywhere else, and particularly in India and Pakistan, crowds flocked to see limited-overs internationals. Test cricket became almost an afterthought. Although the power to change the laws of the game have remained with the MCC, the ICC developed its own Code of Conduct for players, officials, and administrators, which sets out disciplinary procedures and protects the spirit of the game. It also organized major international tournaments, including the one-day and Twenty20 World Cups and the Champions Trophy. In 2000 the ICC set up the Anti-Corruption Unit (renamed the Anti-Corruption Unit and Security Unit in 2003) to combat the growing threat of illegal gambling and match fixing. At the beginning of the 2010.

FIVE

FOOTBALL

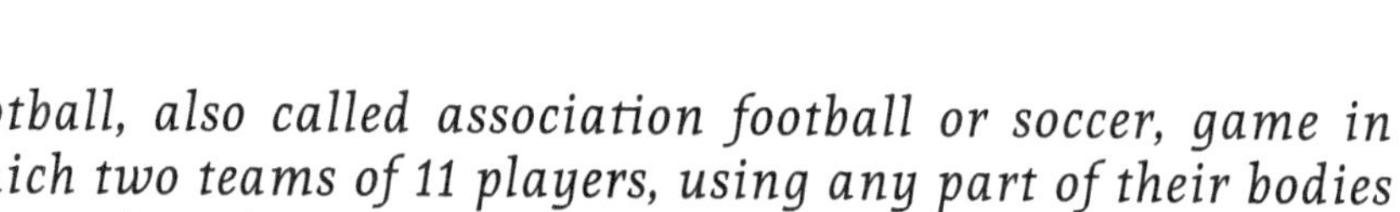

football, also called association football or soccer, game in which two teams of 11 players, using any part of their bodies except their hands and arms, try to maneuver the ball into the opposing team's goal. Only the goalkeeper is permitted to handle the ball and may do so only within the penalty area surrounding the goal. The team that scores more goals wins.

Football is the world's most popular ball game in numbers of participants and spectators. Simple in its principal rules and essential equipment, the sport can be played almost anywhere, from official football playing fields (pitches) to gymnasiums, streets, school playgrounds, parks, or beaches. Football's governing body, the Fédération Internationale de Football Association (FIFA), estimated that at the turn of the 21st century there were approximately 250 million football players and over 1.3 billion people "interested" in football; in 2010 a combined television audience of more than 26 billion watched football's premier tournament, the quadrennial month-long World Cup finals.

History

The early years

Modern football originated in Britain in the 19th century. Since before medieval times, "folk football" games had been played in towns and villages according to local customs and with a minimum of rules. Industrialization and urbanization, which reduced the amount of leisure time and space available to the working class, combined with a history of legal prohibitions against particularly violent and destructive forms of folk football to undermine the game's status from the early 19th century onward. However, football was taken up as a winter game between residence houses at public (independent) schools such as Winchester, Charterhouse, and Eton. Each school had its own rules; some allowed limited handling of the ball and others did not. The variance in rules made it difficult for public schoolboys entering university to continue playing except with former schoolmates. As early as 1843 an attempt to standardize and codify the rules of play was made at the University of Cambridge, whose students joined most public schools in 1848 in adopting these "Cambridge rules," which were further spread by Cambridge graduates who formed football clubs. In 1863 a series of meetings involving clubs from metropolitan London and surrounding counties produced the printed rules of football, which prohibited the carrying of the ball. Thus, the "handling" game of rugby remained outside the newly formed Football Association (FA). Indeed, by 1870 all handling of the ball except by the goalkeeper was prohibited by the FA.

The new rules were not universally accepted in Britain, however; many clubs retained their own rules, especially in and around Sheffield. Although this northern English city was the home of the first provincial club to join the FA, in 1867 it also gave birth to the Sheffield Football Association, the forerunner of later county associations. Sheffield and

London clubs played two matches against each other in 1866, and a year later a match pitting a club from Middlesex against one from Kent and Surrey was played under the revised rules. In 1871 15 FA clubs accepted an invitation to enter a cup competition and to contribute to the purchase of a trophy. By 1877 the associations of Great Britain had agreed upon a uniform code, 43 clubs were in competition, and the London clubs' initial dominance had diminished.

The development of modern football was closely tied to processes of industrialization and urbanization in Victorian Britain. Most of the new working-class inhabitants of Britain's industrial towns and cities gradually lost their old bucolic pastimes, such as badger-baiting, and sought fresh forms of collective leisure. From the 1850s onward, industrial workers were increasingly likely to have Saturday afternoons off work, and so many turned to the new game of football to watch or to play. Key urban institutions such as churches, trade unions, and schools organized working-class boys and men into recreational football teams. Rising adult literacy spurred press coverage of organized sports, while transport systems such as the railways or urban trams enabled players and spectators to travel to football games. Average attendance in England rose from 4,600 in 1888 to 7,900 in 1895, rising to 13,200 in 1905 and reaching 23,100 at the outbreak of World War I. Football's popularity eroded public interest in other sports, notably cricket.

Leading clubs, notably those in Lancashire, started charging admission to spectators as early as the 1870s and so, despite the FA's amateurism rule, were in a position to pay illicit wages to attract highly skilled working-class players, many of them hailing from Scotland. Working-class players and northern English clubs sought a professional system that would provide, in part, some financial reward to cover their "broken time" (time lost from their other work) and the risk of injury. The FA remained staunchly elitist in sustaining a policy of amateurism that protected upper and upper-middle class influence over the game.

The issue of professionalism reached a crisis in England in 1884, when the FA expelled two clubs for using professional players. However, the payment of players had become so commonplace by then that the FA had little option but to sanction the practice a year later, despite initial attempts to restrict professionalism to reimbursements for broken time. The consequence was that northern clubs, with their large supporter bases and capacity to attract better players, came to prominence. As the influence of working-class players rose in football, the upper classes took refuge in other sports, notably cricket and rugby union.

Professionalism also sparked further modernization of the game through the establishment of the Football League, which allowed the leading dozen teams from the North and Midlands to compete systematically against each other from 1888 onward. A lower, second division was introduced in 1893, and the total number of teams increased to 28. The Irish and Scots formed leagues in 1890. The Southern League began in 1894 but was absorbed by the Football League in 1920. Yet football did not become a major profit-making business during this period. Professional clubs became limited liability companies primarily to secure land for gradual development of stadium facilities. Most clubs in England were owned and controlled by businessmen but shareholders received very low, if any, dividends; their main reward was an enhanced public status through running the local club.

Later national leagues overseas followed the British model, which included league championships, at least one annual cup competition, and a hierarchy of leagues that sent clubs finishing highest in the tables (standings) up to the next higher division (promotion) and clubs at the bottom down to the next lower division (relegation). A league was formed in the Netherlands in 1889, but professionalism arrived only in 1954. Germany completed its first national championship season in 1903, but the Bundesliga, a comprehensive and fully professional national league, did not evolve until 60 years later. In France, where the game was introduced in the 1870s, a professional league did not begin until 1932, shortly after professionalism had been adopted in the South American countries of Argentina and Brazil.

International organization

By the early 20th century, football had spread across Europe, but it was in need of international organization. A solution was found in 1904, when representatives from the football associations of Belgium, Denmark, France, the Netherlands, Spain, Sweden, and Switzerland founded the Fédération Internationale de Football Association (FIFA).

2002 World Cup

Although Englishman Daniel Woolfall was elected FIFA president in 1906 and all of the home nations (England, Scotland, Ireland, and Wales) were admitted as members by 1911, British football associations were disdainful of the new body. FIFA members accepted British control over the rules of football via the International Board, which had been established by the home nations in 1882. Nevertheless, in 1920 the British associations resigned their FIFA memberships after failing to persuade other members that Germany, Austria, and Hungary should be expelled following World War I. The British associations rejoined FIFA in 1924 but soon after insisted upon a very rigid definition of amateurism, notably for Olympic football. Other nations again failed to follow their lead, and the British resigned once more in 1928, remaining outside FIFA until 1946. When FIFA established the World Cup championship, British insouciance toward the international game continued. Without membership in FIFA, the British national teams were not invited to the first three competitions (1930, 1934, and 1938). For the next competition, held in 1950, FIFA ruled that the two best finishers in the British home nations tournament would qualify for World Cup play; England won, but Scotland (which finished second) chose not to compete for the World Cup.

Despite sometimes fractious international relations, football continued to rise in popularity. It made its official Olympic debut at the London Games in 1908, and it has since been played in each of the Summer Games (except for the 1932 Games in Los Angeles). FIFA also grew steadily—especially in the latter half of the 20th century, when it strengthened its standing as the game's global authority and regulator of competition. Guinea became FIFA's 100th member in 1961; at the turn of the 21st century, more than 200 nations were registered FIFA members, which is more than the number of countries that belong to the United Nations.

Carli Lloyd

The World Cup finals remain football's premier tournament, but other important tournaments have emerged under FIFA guidance. Two different tournaments for young players began in 1977 and 1985, and these became, respectively, the World Youth Championship (for those 20 years old and younger) and the Under-17 World Championship. Futsal, the world indoor five-a-side championship, started in 1989. Two years later the first Women's World Cup was played in China. In 1992 FIFA opened the Olympic football tournament to players aged under 23 years, and four years later the first women's Olympic football tournament was held. The World Club Championship debuted in Brazil in 2000. The Under-19 Women's World Championship was inaugurated in 2002.

FIFA membership is open to all national associations. They must accept FIFA's authority, observe the laws of football, and possess a suitable football infrastructure (i.e., facilities and internal organization). FIFA statutes require members to form continental confederations. The first of these, the Confederación Sudamericana de Fútbol (commonly known as CONMEBOL), was founded in South America in 1916. In 1954 the Union of European Football Associations (UEFA) and the Asian Football Confederation (AFC) were established. Africa's governing body, the Confédération Africaine de Football (CAF), was founded in 1957. The Confederation of North, Central American and Caribbean Association Football (CONCACAF) followed four years later. The Oceania Football Confederation (OFC) appeared in 1966. These confederations may organize their own club, international, and youth tournaments, elect representatives to FIFA's Executive Committee, and promote football in their specific continents as they see fit. In turn, all football players, agents, leagues, national associations, and confederations must recognize the authority of FIFA's Arbitration Tribunal for Football, which effectively functions as football's supreme court in serious disputes.

Until the early 1970s, control of FIFA (and thus of world football) was firmly in the hands of northern Europeans. Under the presidencies of the Englishmen Arthur Drewry (1955–61) and Stanley Rous (1961–74), FIFA adopted a rather conservative patrician relationship to the national and continental bodies. It survived on modest income from the World Cup finals, and relatively little was done to promote football in developing countries or to explore the game's business potential within the West's postwar economic boom. FIFA's leadership was more concerned with matters of regulation, such as confirming amateur status for Olympic competition or banning those associated with illegal transfers of players with existing contracts. For example, Colombia (1951–54) and Australia (1960–63) were suspended temporarily from FIFA after permitting clubs to recruit players who had broken contracts elsewhere in the world.

Growing African and Asian membership within FIFA undermined European control. In 1974 Brazilian João Havelange was elected president, gaining large support from developing nations. Under Havelange, FIFA was transformed from an international gentlemen's club into a global corporation: billion-dollar television deals and partnerships with major transnational corporations were established during the 1980s and '90s. While some earnings were reinvested through FIFA development projects—primarily in Asia, Africa, and Central America—the biggest political reward for developing countries has been the expansion of the World Cup finals to include more countries from outside Europe and South America.

Greater professionalization of sports also forced FIFA to intercede in new areas as a governing body and competition regulator. The use of performance-enhancing drugs by teams and individual players had been suspected since at least the 1930s; FIFA introduced drug tests in 1966, and occasionally drug users were uncovered, such as Willie Johnston of Scotland at the 1978 World Cup finals. But FIFA regulations were tightened in the 1980s after the sharp rise in offenses among Olympic athletes, the appearance of new drugs such as the steroid nandrolone, and the use of drugs by stars such as Argentina's Diego Maradona in 1994. While FIFA has authorized lengthy worldwide bans of players who fail drug tests, discrepancies remain between nations and confederations over the intensity of testing and the legal status of specific drugs.As the sport moved into the 21st century, FIFA came under pressure to respond to some of the major consequences of globalization for international football. During the corrupt tenure of Switzerland's Sepp Blatter as president from 1998 to 2015, the political bargaining and wrangling among world football's officials gained greater media and public attention. Direct conflicts of interest among football's various groups have also arisen: players, agents, television networks, competition sponsors, *clubs, national bodies, continental associations, and FIFA all have divergent views regarding the staging of football tournaments and the distribution of football's income.*

Regulation of player representatives and transfers is also problematic. In UEFA countries, players move freely when not under contract. On other continents, notably Africa and Central and South America, players tend to be tied into long-term contracts with clubs that can control their entire careers. FIFA now requires all agents to be licensed and to pass written examinations held by national associations, but there is little global consistency regarding the control of agent powers. In Europe, agents have played a key role in promoting wage inflation and higher player mobility. In Latin America, players are often partially "owned" by agents who may decide on whether transfers proceed. In parts of Africa, some European agents have been compared to slave traders in the way that they exercise authoritarian control over players and profit hugely from transfer fees to Western leagues with little thought for their clients' well-being. In this way, the ever-widening inequalities between developed and developing nations are reflected in the uneven growth and variable regulations of world football.

England and Scotland had the first leagues, but clubs sprang up in most European nations in the 1890s and 1900s, enabling these nations to found their own leagues. Many Scottish professional players migrated south to join English clubs, introducing English players and audiences to more-advanced ball-playing skills and to the benefits of teamwork and passing. Up to World War II, the British continued to influence football's development through regular club tours overseas and the Continental coaching careers of former players. Itinerant Scots were particularly prominent in central Europe. The interwar Danubian school of football emerged from the coaching legacies and expertise of John

Madden in Prague and Jimmy Hogan in Austria.

Before World War II, Italian, Austrian, Swiss, and Hungarian teams emerged as particularly strong challengers to the British. During the 1930s, Italian clubs and the Italian national team recruited high-calibre players from South America (mainly Argentina and Uruguay), often claiming that these rimpatriati were essentially Italian in nationality; the great Argentinians Raimondo Orsi and Enrique Guaita were particularly useful acquisitions. But only after World War II was the preeminence of the home nations (notably England) unquestionably usurped by overseas teams. In 1950 England lost to the United States at the World Cup finals in Brazil. Most devastating were later, crushing losses to Hungary: 6–3 in 1953 at London's Wembley Stadium, then 7–1 in Budapest a year later. The "Magical Magyars" opened English eyes to the dynamic attacking and tactically advanced football played on the Continent and to the technical superiority of players such as Ferenc Puskás, József Bozsik, and Nándor Hidegkuti. During the 1950s and '60s, Italian and Spanish clubs were the most active in the recruitment of top foreign players. For example, the Welshman John Charles, known as "the Gentle Giant," remains a hero for supporters of the Juventus club of Turin, Italy, while the later success of Real Madrid was built largely on the play of Argentinian Alfredo Di Stefano and the Hungarian Puskás.

European football has also reflected the wider political, economic, and cultural changes of modern times. Heightened nationalism and xenophobia have pervaded matches, often as a harbinger of future hostilities. During the 1930s, international matches in Europe were often seen as national tests of physical and military capability. In contrast, football's early post-World War II boom witnessed massive, well-behaved crowds that coincided with Europe's shift from warfare to rebuilding projects and greater internationalism. More recently, racism became a more prominent feature of football, particularly during the 1970s and early 1980s: many coaches projected negative stereotypes onto Black players; supporters routinely abused nonwhites on and off the fields of play; and football authorities failed to counteract racist incidents at games. In general terms, racism at football reflected wider social problems across western Europe. In postcommunist eastern Europe, economic decline and rising nationalist sentiments have marked football culture too. The tensions that exploded in Yugoslavia's civil war were foreshadowed during a match in May 1990 between the Serbian side Red Star Belgrade and the Croatian team Dynamo Zagreb when violence involving rival supporters and Serbian riot police spread to the pitch to include players and coaches.

Club football reflects the distinctive political and cultural complexities of European regions. In Britain, partisan football has been traditionally associated with the industrial working class, notably in cities such as Glasgow, Liverpool, Manchester, and Newcastle. In Spain, clubs such as FC Barcelona and Athletic Bilbao are symbols of strong nationalist identity for Catalans and Basques, respectively. In France, many clubs have facilities that are open to the local community and reflect the nation's corporatist politics in being jointly owned and administered by private investors and local governments. In Italy, clubs such as Fiorentina, Inter Milan, SSC Napoli, and AS Roma embody deep senses of civic and regional pride that predate Italian unification in the 19th century.

The dominant forces in European national football have been Germany, Italy, and, latterly, France; their national teams have won a total of seven World Cups and six European Championships. Success in club football has been built largely on recruitment of the world's leading players, notably by Italian and Spanish sides. The European Cup competition for national league champions, first played in 1955, was initially dominated by Real Madrid; other regular winners have been AC Milan, Bayern Munich (Germany), Ajax of Amsterdam, and Liverpool FC (England). The UEFA Cup, first contested as the Fairs Cup in 1955–58, has had a wider pool of entrants and winners.

Since the late 1980s, topflight European football has generated increasing financial revenues from higher ticket prices, merchandise sales, sponsorship, advertising, and, in particular, television contracts. The top professionals and largest clubs have been the principal beneficiaries. UEFA has reinvented the European Cup as the Champions League, allowing the wealthiest clubs freer entry and more matches. In the early 1990s, Belgian player Jean-Marc Bosman sued the Belgian Football Association, challenging European football's traditional rule that all transfers of players (including those without contracts) necessitate an agreement between the clubs in question, usually involving a transfer fee. Bosman had been prevented from joining a new club (US Dunkerque) by his old club (RC Liège). In 1995 the European courts upheld Bosman's complaint, and at a stroke freed uncontracted European players to move between clubs without transfer fees.

The bargaining power of players was strengthened greatly, enabling top stars to multiply their earnings with large salaries and signing bonuses. Warnings of the end of European football's financial boom came when FIFA's marketing agent, ISL, went bust in 2001; such major media investors in football as the Kirch Gruppe in Germany and ITV Digital in the United Kingdom collapsed a year later. Inevitably, the financial boom had exacerbated inequalities within the game, widening the gap between the top players, the largest clubs, and the wealthiest spectators and their *counterparts in lower leagues and the developing world.*

North and Central America and the Caribbean

Football was brought to North America in the 1860s, and by the mid-1880s informal matches had been contested by Canadian and American teams. It soon faced competition from other sports, including variant forms of football. In Canada, Scottish émigrés were particularly prominent in the game's early development; however, Canadians subsequently turned to ice hockey as their national sport.

In the United States, gridiron football emerged early in the 20th century as the most popular sport. But, beyond elite universities and schools, soccer (as the sport is popularly called in the United States) was played widely in some cities with large immigrant populations such as Philadelphia, Chicago, Cleveland (Ohio), and St. Louis (Missouri), as well as New York City and Los Angeles after Hispanic migrations. The U.S. Soccer Federation formed in 1913, affiliated with FIFA, and sponsored competitions. Between the world wars, the United States attracted scores of European emigrants who played football for local teams sometimes sponsored by companies.

Football in Central America struggled to gain a significant foothold in competition against baseball. In Costa Rica, the football federation founded the national league championship in 1921, but subsequent development in the region was slower, with belated FIFA membership for countries such as El Salvador (1938), Nicaragua (1950), and Honduras (1951). In the Caribbean, football traditionally paled in popularity to cricket in former British colonies. In Jamaica, football was highly popular in urban townships, but it did not capture the imagination of the country until 1998, when the national team—featuring several players who had gained success in Britain and were dubbed the "Reggae Boyz"—qualified for the World Cup finals.

North American leagues and tournaments saw an infusion of professional players in 1967, beginning with the wholesale importation of foreign teams to represent American cities. The North American Soccer League (NASL) formed a year later and struggled until the New York Cosmos signed the Brazilian superstar Pelé in 1975. Other aging international stars soon followed, and crowds grew to European proportions, but a regular fan base remained elusive, and NASL folded in 1985. An indoor football tournament, founded in 1978, evolved into a league and flourished for a while but collapsed in 1992.

In North America football did establish itself as the relatively less-violent alternative to gridiron football and as a more socially inclusive sport for women. It is particularly popular among college and high school students across the United States. After hosting an entertaining World Cup finals in 1994, the United States possessed some 16 million football players nationwide, up to 40 percent of whom were female. In 1996 a new attempt at establishing a professional outdoor league was made. Major League Soccer (MLS) was more modest in ambition than NASL, being originally played in only 10 U.S. cities, with greater emphasis on local players and a relatively tight salary cap. The MLS proved to be the most successful American soccer league, expanding to 20 teams (with two in Canada) by 2016 while also signing a number of lucrative broadcasting deals with American television networks and some star players from European leagues. The United States hosted and won the Women's World Cup finals in 1999, attracting enthusiastic local support. The success of the MLS and the Women's World Cup led to the creation of a women's professional league in 2001. The Women's United Soccer Association (WUSA) began with eight teams and featured the world's star player, Mia Hamm, but it disbanded in 2003.

North American national associations are members of the continental body, CONCACAF, and Mexico is the traditional regional powerhouse. Mexico has won the CONCACAF Gold Cup four times since it was first contested in 1991, and Mexican clubs have dominated the CONCACAF Champions Cup for clubs since it began in 1962. British influence in mining and railroads encouraged the founding of football clubs in Mexico in the late 19th century. A national league was established in 1903. Mexico is exceptional in that its mass preference for football runs counter to the sporting tastes of its North American neighbours.

The national league system is the most commercially successful in the region and attracts players from all over the Western Hemisphere. Despite high summer humidity and stadiums at high elevations, Mexico has hosted two of the most memorable World Cup finals, in 1970 and 1986, from which Brazil and Argentina (led by the game's then greatest players, Pelé and Maradona, respectively) emerged as the respective winners. While the national team has been ranked highly by FIFA, often figuring in the top ten, Mexico initially did not produce the world-class calibre of players expected of such a large football-crazed nation. Hugo Sanchez (at Real Madrid) was the only Mexican player to reach the highest world level in the 20th century, but the 21st saw a number of Mexican standouts excel with top European clubs.

South America

Football first came to South America in the 19ᵗʰ century through the port of Buenos Aires, Argentina, where European sailors played the game. Members of the British community there formed the first club, the Buenos Aires Football Club (FC), in 1867; about the same time, British railway workers started another club, in the town of Rosario, Argentina. The first Argentinian league championship was played in 1893, but most of the players belonged to the British community, a pattern that continued until the early 20ᵗʰ century.

Brazil is believed to be the second South American country where the game was established. Charles Miller, a leading player in England, came to Brazil in 1894 and introduced football in São Paulo; that city's athletic club was the first to take up the sport. In Colombia, British engineers and workers building a railroad near Barranquilla first played football in 1903, and the Barranquilla FBC was founded in 1909. In Uruguay, British railway workers were the first to play, and in 1891 they founded the Central Uruguay Railway Cricket Club (now the famous Peñarol), which played both cricket and football. In Chile, British sailors initiated play in Valparaíso, establishing the Valparaíso FC in 1889. In Paraguay, Dutchman William Paats introduced the game at a school where he taught physical education, but the country's first (and still leading) club, Olimpia, was formed by a local man who became enthusiastic after seeing the game in Buenos Aires in 1902. In Bolivia the first footballers were a Chilean and students who had studied in Europe, and in Peru they were expatriate Britons. In Venezuela, British miners are known to have played football in the 1880s.

Soon local people across South America began taking up and following the sport in ever greater numbers. Boys, mostly from poorer backgrounds, played from an early age, with passion, on vacant land and streets. Clubs and players gained popularity, and professionalism entered the sport in most countries around the 1930s—although many players had been paid secretly before then by their clubs. The exodus of South American players to European clubs that paid higher salaries began after the 1930 World Cup and has steadily increased.

Africa

European sailors, soldiers, traders, engineers, and missionaries brought football with them to Africa in the second half of the 19th century. The first documented match took place in Cape Town in 1862, after which the game spread rapidly throughout the continent, particularly in the British colonies and in societies with vibrant indigenous athletic traditions.

During the interwar period, African men in cities and towns, railroad workers, and students organized clubs, associations, and regional competitions. Teams from Algeria, Morocco, and Tunisia competed in the North African championship, established in 1919, and vied for the North African Cup, introduced in 1930. South of the Sahara, Kenya and Uganda first played for the Gossage Trophy in 1924, and the Darugar Cup was established on the island of Zanzibar. In the mining centre of Élisabethville (now Lubumbashi, Congo) a football league for Africans was begun in 1925. In South Africa the game was very popular by the early 1930s, though it was organized in racially segregated national associations for whites, Africans, Coloureds (persons of mixed race), and Indians. In the colonies of British West Africa, the Gold Coast (now Ghana) launched its first football association in 1922, with Nigeria's southern capital of Lagos following suit in 1931. Enterprising clubs and leagues developed across French West Africa in the 1930s, especially in Senegal and Côte d'Ivoire. Moroccan forward Larbi Ben Barek became the first

African professional in Europe, playing for Olympique de Marseille and the French national team in 1938.

After World War II football in Africa experienced dramatic expansion. Modernizing colonial regimes provided new facilities and created attractive competitions, such as the French West Africa Cup in 1947. The migration of talented Africans to European clubs intensified. Together with his older compatriot Mario Coluña, Mozambican sensation Eusébio, European player of the year in 1965, starred for European champions Benfica of Lisbon and led Portugal to third place in the 1966 World Cup, where he was the tournament's leading scorer. Algerian stars Rachid Mekhloufi of Saint-Étienne and Mustafa Zitouni of AS Monaco represented France before joining the team of the Algerian National Liberation Front (FLN) in 1958. The FLN eleven, who lost only 4 of 58 matches during the period 1958–62, embodied the close relations between nationalist movements and football in Africa on the eve of decolonization.

With colonialism's hold on Africa slipping away, the Confédération Africaine de Football (CAF) was established in February 1957 in Khartoum, Sudan, with the first African Cup of Nations tournament also played at that time. Independent African states encouraged football as a means of forging a national identity and generating international recognition.

In the 1960s and early '70s, African football earned a reputation for a spectacular, attacking style of play. African and European coaches emphasized craft, creativity, and fitness within solid but flexible tactical schemes. Salif Keita (Mali), Laurent Pokou (Côte d'Ivoire), and François M'Pelé (Congo [Brazzaville]) personified the dynamic qualities of football in postcolonial Africa.

In the late 1970s, the migration of talented players overseas began hampering domestic leagues. The effects of this player exodus were somewhat tempered by the rise of "scientific football" and defensive, risk-averting tactics, an international trend that saw African players fall out of favour with European clubs. Even so, the integration of Africa and Africans into world football accelerated in the 1980s and '90s. Cameroon's national team, known as the Indomitable Lions, was a driving force in this process. After being eliminated without losing a match at the 1982 World Cup in Spain (tied with Italy in its group, Cameroon lost the tiebreaker on the basis of total goals scored), Cameroon reached the quarterfinals at the 1990 World Cup in Italy, thereby catapulting African football into the global spotlight. Nigeria then captured the Olympic gold medal in men's football at the Summer Games in Atlanta in 1996; in 2000 Cameroon won its first Olympic gold medal in men's football at the Games in Sydney, Australia. Success also came at youth level as Nigeria (1985) and Ghana (1991 and 1995) claimed under-17 world titles. Moreover, Liberian striker George Weah of Paris St. Germain received the prestigious FIFA World Player of the Year award in 1995.

In recognition of African football's success and influence, FIFA awarded Africa five places in the 32-team 1998 World Cup finals. This achievement bears witness to African football's phenomenal passion, growth, and development. This rich and complex history is made more remarkable by the continent's struggles to cope with a fragile environment, scarce material resources, political conflicts, and the unpleasant legacy of imperialism.

Asia and Oceania

Football quickly entered Asia and Oceania in the latter half of the 19th century, but, unlike in Europe, it failed to become a unifying national sport. In Australia it could not dislodge the winter games of Australian rules football (codified before soccer) and rugby. British immigrants to Australia did relatively little to develop football locally. Because southern European immigrants were more committed to founding clubs and tournaments, football became defined as an "ethnic game." As a result, teams from Melbourne and Sydney with distinctive Mediterranean connections were the most prominent members of the National Soccer League (NSL) when it started in 1977. The league has widened its scope, however, to include a highly successful Perth side, plus a Brisbane club and even one from Auckland, New Zealand. The NSL collapsed in 2004, but a new league, known as the A-League, emerged the next year.

In New Zealand, Scottish players established clubs and tournaments from the 1880s, but rugby became the national passion. In Asia, during the same germinal period, British traders, engineers, and teachers set up football clubs in such colonial outposts as Shanghai, Hong Kong, Singapore, and Burma (Myanmar). Yet football's major problem across Asia, until the 1980s, was its failure to establish substantial roots among indigenous peoples beyond college students returning from Europe. Football in India was particularly prominent in Calcutta (Kolkata) among British soldiers, but locals soon adopted cricket. In Japan, Yokohama and Kobe housed large numbers of football-playing foreigners, but local people retained preferences for the traditional sport of sumo wrestling and the imported game of baseball.

At the turn of the 21ˢᵗ century, football became increasingly important in Asian societies. In Iran, national team football matches became opportunities for many to express their reformist political views as well as for broad public celebration. The Iraqi men's team's fourth-place finish at the 2004 Olympic Games in Athens struck a chord of hope for their war-torn homeland.

The Asian game is organized by the Asian Football Confederation, comprising 46 members in 2011 and stretching geographically from Lebanon in the Middle East to Guam in the western Pacific Ocean. The Asian Cup for national teams has been held quadrennially since 1956; Iran, Saudi Arabia, and Japan have dominated, with South Korea a regular runner-up. These countries have also produced the most frequent winners of the annual Asian Club Championship, first contested in 1967.

Asian economic growth during the 1980s and early 1990s and greater cultural ties to the West helped cultivate club football. Japan's J-League was launched in 1993, attracting strong public interest and a sprinkling of famous foreign players and coaches (notably from South America). Attendance and revenue declined from 1995, but the league survived and was reorganized into two divisions of 16 and 10 clubs, respectively, by 1999. The league grew to 30 teams by 2005 but had reduced to 18 by 2018.

Some memorable international moments have indicated the potential of football in Asia and Oceania. Asia's first notable success was North Korea's stunning defeat of Italy at the 1966 World Cup finals. In 1994 Saudi Arabia became the first Asian team to qualify for the World Cup's second round. The entertaining 2002 World Cup hosted by Japan and South Korea and the on-field success of the host nations' national teams (South Korea reached the semifinals; Japan reached the second round) stood as the region's brightest accomplishment in international football.

Football's future in Asia and Oceania depends largely upon regular competition with top international teams and players. Increased representation in the World Cup finals (since 1998 Asia has sent four teams, and since 2006 Oceania has had a single automatic berth) has helped development of the sport in the region. Meanwhile, domestic club competitions across Asia and Oceania have been weakened by the need for top national players to join better clubs in Europe or South America to test and improve their talents at a markedly higher level. One promising development for the continent came in 2010 when Qatar was announced as the host of the 2022 World Cup, which will be the first World Cup held in the Middle East.

SIX
KABADDI

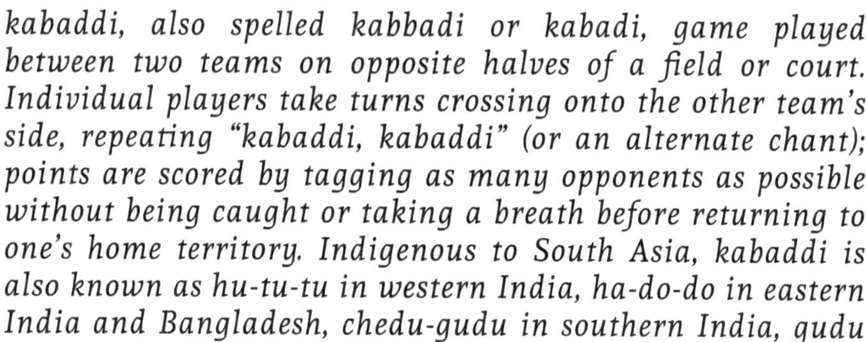

kabaddi, also spelled kabbadi or kabadi, game played between two teams on opposite halves of a field or court. Individual players take turns crossing onto the other team's side, repeating "kabaddi, kabaddi" (or an alternate chant); points are scored by tagging as many opponents as possible without being caught or taking a breath before returning to one's home territory. Indigenous to South Asia, kabaddi is also known as hu-tu-tu in western India, ha-do-do in eastern India and Bangladesh, chedu-gudu in southern India, gudu in Sri Lanka, and theechub in Thailand.

It has been speculated that the game originated in prehistoric times, when the development of human reflexes was crucial for self-defense and hunting. The ancient Indian epic poem Mahabharata, in its account of the legendary battles of Kurukshetra, tells of a military operation—a doomed raid by Arjuna's son, Abhimanyu, on an enemy camp—that has been noted for its resemblance to kabaddi. For many years kabaddi was played for physical exercise by pupils in Indian gurukuls (Vedic schools run by gurus). Though minor variations emerged, the game's principal objective of raiding the enemy territory remained common.

The basic rules of kabaddi were formalized in India in the early 20th *century and published in 1923. The game received international exposure when it was demonstrated by an Amravati-based sports organization at the 1936 Olympic Games in Berlin, and it was included as an event in the Indian Olympic Games held in Calcutta (now Kolkata) two years later. Following its formation in 1950, the Kabaddi Federation of India organized national championships for men beginning in 1952 and for women beginning in 1955. In the late 20*[th] *century the popularity of organized kabaddi began to expand beyond India's borders, in part through the efforts of the Amateur Kabaddi Federation of India, formed in 1972. That same year kabaddi was designated the national game of Bangladesh. With the establishment in 1978 of the Asian Amateur Kabaddi Federation, a regional championship was organized, and national kabaddi teams began to compete in the Asian Games in 1990.*

By the early 21st *century international competition typically involved seven players per team performing on a rectangular court, although other styles (such as "circular" kabaddi) remained popular in India and elsewhere. The first Kabaddi World Cup, staged in Mumbai (Bombay) in 2004, hosted national teams from Asia, Europe, and North America.*

With a 4000-year-long history, the traditional Indian sport of kabaddi is one of the oldest in the world.

Showcased as an exhibition sport on the sidelines of the Berlin 1936 Olympics, kabaddi's popularity has soared by leaps and bounds over the years. After appearing as a demonstration sport at the Asian Games in 1951 and 1982, kabaddi finally became a medal event at the continental showpiece from 1990 and has been a permanent fixture since then.

The Asian Games 2022 in Hangzhou, China will also see kabaddi in the main program.

Kabaddi is fast, furious and physical, making for a great spectacle – a fact vindicated by the ever-rising global popularity of Pro Kabaddi, a franchise-based kabaddi league which started in India in 2014.

For anyone new to the sport, here's a basic guideline to kabaddi rules and how to play the sport.

Kabaddi mat: Dimensions and markings

To understand kabaddi, one needs to first have a basic layout of a kabaddi mat.In each half, there are two more lines drawn parallel to the mid line. The baulk line is at a distance of 3.75m from the mid line while the bonus line is drawn 1m further back from the baulk line (between the baulk line and the end line).

Two lines, 1m inside the longer boundaries, run through the entire length of the mat, creating two channels on the mat which are called lobbies. Lobbies are sometimes marked with a different colour on the mat.Though traditionally played on soft muddy fields, most popular competitive kabaddi events are currently played on rectangular padded kabaddi mats.Kabaddi mat dimensions may vary according to tournaments and age groups, but it mostly measures 13m x 10m for senior men's professional kabaddi events. The mat is slightly smaller, 12m x 8m, for women.The four outer lines of the kabaddi mat are called boundaries or end lines. The play needs to be restricted within the four boundary lines at any time.The rectangular court is divided into two equal identical halves by a mid line, drawn parallelly to the shorter end lines of the mat.

A kabaddi match typically runs for 40 minutes (two halves of 20 minutes each).The match starts with a coin toss between the two teams and the winner can decide whether to raid or defend first.Each team is allowed two time-outs in each half.Each team in a kabaddi match has seven players. The teams can also have three to five substitute players on the bench.

A kabaddi match starts with one team raiding the other team's half.

During a raid, any one player from the attacking team, called the raider, enters the other team's half while chanting the word kabaddi, also known as canting.

The objective of the raider is to tag or touch as many opposition players, called antis or defenders, as possible and return to their own half by crossing the mid line while continuing their cant under one breath.

The defenders, meanwhile, try to stop the raider from returning to his own half by tackling or pushing him out of the court.

A raider has two avenues to score points during a raid.

He can either go for touch points, which means he tags one or more of the opposition players and successfully escapes to his own half without breaking the cant.

If touch points are scored, the antis or defenders who had been tagged during the raid have to exit the mat. Raiders earn as many touch points as the number of players they eliminate during a raid.

The eliminated players, however, can be revived and brought back into the game if a raider from their team scores touch points on the opposition team during a subsequent raid or their team can pull off a successful raid on the opposition raider as the match progresses.

Revivals happen in the same sequence as eliminations.

Similarly, a raider is also out of the game if they are tackled by the opposition defenders during a raid. A successful tackle earns the defending team one point, also called points earned through defending are often termed as tackle points in modern kabaddi.

If a raider loses his cant during a raid, he's also out and the defending team earns a point.

If a team can eliminate all seven players of the opposition team, they earn two extra points via all out or Lona. After a team scores a Lona, all members of the opposition team are revived and play resumes.

Do note, a raider can also safely return without getting eliminated if they can cross the baulk line (either have both foot across the baulk line or have one foot across the baulk line while their other foot is on the air). A safe return by just crossing the baulk line, however, doesn't result in points won or revivals and are termed as empty raids.The other way for raiders to score is through bonus points. To score a bonus point, a raider needs to plant one foot across the bonus line while having the trailing foot on air. Bonus points, however, are only active when the defending team has six or more players on the mat.

Also, during the entire sequence of play, if a defender or raider steps outside the boundary line, they are out and the opposition team gets a point and a revival. The lobby area is also out of bounds of play until a defender makes contact with the raider – also called a struggle.Stepping onto the lobby before a struggle initiates results in the same penalties as stepping outside the boundaries of the mat.If a knockout kabaddi match ends in a tie, a seven-minute-long mini match, with two halves, is played to determine the winner. If the extra time fails to establish a winner, the match is decided by a sudden-death Golden Raid, where the baulk line moves up to the baulk line.If there's a draw even after the Golden Raid, the winner is established by coin toss.

SEVEN

BADMINTON

badminton, court or lawn game played with lightweight rackets and a shuttlecock. Historically, the shuttlecock (also known as a "bird" or "birdie") was a small cork hemisphere with 16 goose feathers attached and weighing about 0.17 ounce (5 grams). These types of shuttles may still be used in modern play, but shuttles made from synthetic materials are also allowed by the Badminton World Federation. The game is named for Badminton, the country estate of the dukes of Beaufort in Gloucestershire, England, where it was first played about 1873. The roots of the sport can be traced to ancient Greece, China, and India, and it is closely related to the old children's game battledore and shuttlecock. Badminton is derived directly from poona, which was played by British army officers stationed in India in the 1860s. The first unofficial all-England badminton championships for men were held in 1899, and the first badminton tournament for women was arranged the next year.

The Badminton World Federation (BWF; originally the International Badminton Federation), the world governing body of the sport, was formed in 1934. Badminton is also popular in Malaysia, Indonesia, Japan, and Denmark. The BWF's first world championships were held in 1977. A number of regional, national, and zonal badminton *tournaments are held in several countries. The best-known of these is the All-England Championships. Other well-known international tournaments include the Thomas Cup (donated 1939) for men's team competition and the Uber Cup (donated 1956) for women's team competition.*

Badminton is set to be one of the big draws at Tokyo 2020 with two-time defending world champion Kento Momota hoping to win Japan's second Olympic title in the sport.

Chen Long and Carolina Marin will defend their singles titles in Japan with golds also up for grabs in men's doubles, women's doubles and mixed doubles.While badminton is most popular in Asia, it also attracts great interest in Europe with players from Denmark among those regularly challenging for top honours.Want to learn more about badminton? Here's a look at the rules and equipment you need to play, plus a brief history of the sport at the Olympic Games.As outlined by the Badminton World Federation

(BWF), *here is a simplified rundown of the rules of badminton.*

All singles and doubles matches are the best-of-three games. The first side to 21 points wins a game.A point is scored on every serve and awarded to whichever side wins the rally. The winning side gets the next serve.If the score is 20-20, a side must win by two clear points to win the game. If it reaches 29-29, the first to get their 30th point wins.

A point is won if the birdie (shuttlecock) hits the ground in the opponent's half of the court, including the lines.A point can therefore be conceded if a shot goes outside the court boundaries, if the birdie hits the net or passes through/under it, or if a player strikes the birdie twice with their racket.Players must wait for the birdie to cross the net before playing a shot, and while you can follow through over it, touching the net with your body or racket results in a point being conceded.

The birdie must be hit below waist height, with players serving diagonally into their opponent's service box. Both players must remain stationary until the serve is made.In singles, the server starts from the right service court, and will serve from that side every time they have an even amount of points. A player serves from the left every time they have an odd amount of points.Each player will retain serve for as long as they keep winning points.In doubles, the server will start on the right-hand side and keep serving, while alternating sides with their team-mate, so long as they keep winning points.If the receiving side takes the point, they assume serve. Going forward, the player who did not initially serve for each team will only assume the service once their side has won a point as the receiving side.

In singles, a badminton court is 13.41m (44ft) long and 5.18m (17ft) wide. The width extends to 6.1m (20ft) in doubles. The net is 1.55m (5ft 1in) high at the ends and 1.52m high (5ft) where it dips in the middle. A serve must pass the short service line, which is 1.98m (6.5ft) from the net. Beyond the short service line, there is a line which runs down the middle to split the left and right service courts. There is also a doubles service line 0.76m (2.5ft) in from the baseline. That means each service court (four in total) is 3.96m (13ft) long and 2.59m (8.5ft) wide.

The birdie, also referred to as the shuttlecock, is badminton's unique 'ball'.

The cone-shaped projectile is formed using feathers or a synthetic material which are attached to a cork or rubber base. The birdie's shape means it will always fly cork-first once struck, and remain so until hit again. Made up of 16 feathers, the birdie is between 62-70mm long and weigh between 4.74 and 5.5g. The tip of the feathers should create a circle with a diameter from 58-62mm, with the cork/rubber base 25-28mm in diameter and rounded at the bottom.

A regular fixture since the Barcelona 1992 Summer Olympics, badminton now has five disciplines at the Games after mixed doubles was introduced at Atlanta 1996.

Indonesia claimed both singles golds on badminton's Olympic debut courtesy of Alan Budikusuma and Susi Susanti, with Republic of Korea taking the two doubles titles on offer. China has since emerged as the sport's dominant force with a total of 18 gold, eight silver and 15 bronze medals ahead of Tokyo 2020. Korea is second with seven gold, six silver and six bronze medals, with Indonesia third on six gold, seven silver and six bronze medals.Denmark, Japan and Spain have one gold apiece with India looking to women's world champion and Rio 2016 silver medallist PV Sindhu to earn her nation's first badminton Olympic title.Ten players have won two Olympic gold medals but just two of them have a brace of singles titles - 2004 and 2008 women's champion Zhang Ning and Lin Dan who retained his men's crown at London 2012 by repeating his Beijing 2008 triumph over Lee Chong Wei.Gao Ling is badminton's only four-time Olympic medallist thanks to two mixed doubles golds in 2000 and 2004, and bronze and silver in women's doubles at those Games.

EIGHT

HOCKEY

Until the mid-1980s it was generally accepted that ice hockey derived from English field hockey and Indian lacrosse and was spread throughout Canada by British soldiers in the mid-1800s. Research then turned up mention of a hockeylike game, played in the early 1800s in Nova Scotia by the Mi'kmaq (Micmac) Indians, which appeared to have been heavily influenced by the Irish game of hurling; it included the use of a "hurley" (stick) and a square wooden block instead of a ball. It was probably fundamentally this game that spread throughout Canada via Scottish and Irish immigrants and the British army. The players adopted elements of field hockey, such as the "bully" (later the face-off) and "shinning" (hitting one's opponent on the shins with the stick or playing with the stick on one "shin" or side); this evolved into an informal ice game later known as shinny or shinty. The name hockey—as the organized game came to be known—has been attributed to the French word hoquet (shepherd's stick). The term rink, referring to the designated area of play, was originally used in the game of curling in 18th-century Scotland. Early hockey games allowed as many as 30 players a side on the ice, and the goals were two stones, each frozen into one end of the ice. The first use of a puck instead of a ball was recorded at Kingston Harbour, Ontario, Canada, in 1860.

Early organization

The first recorded public indoor ice hockey game, with rules largely borrowed from field hockey, took place in Montreal's Victoria Skating Rink in 1875 between two teams of McGill University students. Unfortunately, the reputation for violence that the game would later develop was presaged in this early encounter, where, as The Daily British Whig of Kingston, Ontario, reported, "Shins and heads were battered, benches smashed and the lady spectators fled in confusion." The first organized team, the McGill University Hockey Club, formed in 1877, codified their game's rules and limited the number of players on a side to nine.

By the late 1800s ice hockey competed with lacrosse as Canada's most popular sport. The first national hockey organization, the Amateur Hockey Association (AHA) of Canada (which limited players to seven a side), was formed in Montreal in 1885, and the first league was formed in Kingston during the same year, with four teams: the Kingston Hockey Club, Queen's University, the Kingston Athletics, and the Royal Military College. Queen's University scored a 3–1 victory over the Athletics in the first championship game.

By the opening of the 20th century, sticks were being manufactured, shin pads were worn, the goaltender began to wear a chest protector (borrowed from baseball), and arenas (still with natural ice and no heat for spectators) were being constructed throughout eastern Canada. In 1893 national attention was focused on the game when the Canadian governor-general, Frederick Arthur, Lord Stanley of Preston, donated a cup to be given annually to the top Canadian team. The three-foot-high silver cup became known as the Stanley Cup and was first awarded in 1892–93. (The first winner was *the Montreal Amateur Athletic Association team, which also captured the Stanley Cup the following season by winning the initial challenge series to determine the Cup holder, which was the Cup-awarding format that Lord Stanley originally intended.) Since 1926 the cup has gone to the winner of the National Hockey League play-offs.*

In 1899 the Canadian Amateur Hockey League was formed. All hockey in Canada at the time was "amateur," it being "ungentlemanly" to admit to being paid for athletic services. Thus, the first acknowledged professional hockey team in the world was formed in the United States, in 1903, in Houghton, Michigan. The team, the Portage Lakers, was owned by a dentist named J.L. Gibson, who imported Canadian players. In 1904 Gibson formed the first acknowledged professional league, the International Pro Hockey League. Canada accepted professional hockey in 1908 when the Ontario Professional Hockey League was formed. By that time Canada had become the centre of world hockey.The National Hockey Association (NHA), the forerunner of the National Hockey League (NHL), was organized in 1910 and became the

strongest hockey association in North America. Rising interest in the game created problems, however, for there were few artificial-ice rinks. In 1911 the Pacific Coast Hockey Association (PCHA) was formed by Joseph Patrick and his sons, who built two enclosed artificial-ice arenas, beginning a boom in the construction of artificial-ice rinks.The PCHA became involved in a money and player war with the NHA.

Although the NHA ultimately emerged as the stronger league, it was the PCHA that introduced many of the changes that improved the game. The only radical rule change adopted by the NHA was to reduce the number of players on a side to six, and that move was made to save money. The western league retained seven-man hockey, but it allowed the goalie to leap or dive to stop the puck. Under the previous rules, a goalie had had to remain stationary when making a save. The western league also changed the offside rule. Under the old rules, a player had been deemed offside if he was ahead of the puck carrier when he received a pass. The PCHA divided the ice into three zones by painting two blue lines across the surface and allowed forward passing in the centre zone between the blue lines. This opened up the game and made it more exciting. Another innovation in the western league was the idea of the assist. Previously, only the goal scorer had been credited with a point. In the PCHA the player or players who set up his goal were credited with an assist. The first numbered uniforms also appeared in their league.

The National Hockey League

Like some of its predecessors, the NHA had its dissenters. In a move to eject one of the league members, the NHA decided to disband and form a new league. The result was the creation in 1917 of the National Hockey League (NHL), which became the world's foremost professional hockey league. In 1924 the *first U.S. team, the Boston Bruins, joined the NHL. In 1925 the New York Americans and Pittsburgh Pirates were admitted, followed in 1926 by the New York Rangers, the Chicago Blackhawks, and the Detroit Cougars (later called the Red Wings). To stock the new teams, the NHL bought out the Patricks' league in 1926 for $250,000. Among the players who shifted to Boston was Eddie Shore, known as a "rushing" defenseman, whose style helped change the game. He was one of the sport's most ferocious and, many experts say, most skilled players, a forerunner of such future NHL players as Gordie Howe, who played mostly for the Detroit Red Wings. The Pittsburgh Pirates and the New York Americans eventually dropped out of the league, and, until the expansion of 1967, the NHL was composed of only six teams: the Rangers, the Bruins, the Blackhawks, the Red Wings, the Toronto Maple Leafs, and the Montreal Canadiens.*

In 1967 the NHL undertook one of the greatest expansions in professional sports history when it doubled in size to 12 teams. A new 12-team league, the World Hockey Association (WHA), was formed in 1972, and the ensuing rivalry caused an escalation in players' salaries. In 1979 the NHL, which had grown to 17 teams, merged with the WHA to become a 21-team league; by 2017, 31 teams played in the NHL. In 2004, owners locked out players, insisting that they accept a salary cap that would slow the rapid growth of payroll costs. The players rejected the owners' demands, and the entire 2004–05 season was canceled. (The league resumed play in 2005–06 after the owners ultimately prevailed, and the NHL became the last of the major North American team-sport leagues to institute a salary cap.) The regular season consists of 82 games and determines the 16 teams that will qualify for the play-offs. The play-off winner is awarded the Stanley Cup.

NHL individual awards are the Vezina Trophy, for the goalie voted best at his position by NHL managers; the William

M. Jennings Trophy, for the goalie or goalies with the team permitting the fewest goals; the Calder Memorial Trophy, for the rookie of the year; the Hart Memorial Trophy, for the most valuable player; the James Norris Memorial Trophy, for the outstanding defenseman; the Art Ross Trophy, for the top point scorer; the Lady Byng Memorial Trophy, for the player best combining clean play with a high degree of skill; the Conn Smythe Trophy, for the play-offs' outstanding performer; the Frank J. Selke Trophy, for the best defensive forward; the Jack Adams Award, for the coach of the year; the Bill Masterton Memorial Trophy, for the player who best exemplifies sportsmanship, perseverance, and dedication to hockey; and the Lester Patrick Trophy, for outstanding service to U.S. hockey.

International ice hockey

For much of the 20th century, amateur athletes dominated international competition. League competition among amateurs in England began in 1903. The International Ice Hockey Federation (IIHF) was formed in Europe in 1908. Its five original members were Great Britain, Bohemia, Switzerland, France, and Belgium. The first European championship was held at Avants, Switzerland, in 1910, with Great Britain the winner. From that time the federation broadened its membership, taking applicants from the world over. Canada captured the first Olympic Games title in 1920 and, concurrently, the first IIHF world championship. Canada, which also won at the first Olympic Winter Games in 1924, dominated international competition until the emergence of the Soviet team in the early 1960s. The Soviets continued to be the most powerful team in international hockey until the 1990s and the dissolution of the Soviet Union.

Rules and principles of play

The modern game on every level—amateur, collegiate, international, and professional—has been influenced largely by the NHL.

Checking—body contact to take an opponent out of play—is permitted anywhere on the ice. In most leagues, including the NHL, players may not make or take a pass that has traveled across the two blue lines; if this occurs, the play is ruled offside. A face-off, in which an official drops the puck between opposing players, follows the infraction. Face-offs are held at the point of the infraction. Players who precede the puck into the attacking zone also are ruled offside, and a face-off is held at a face-off spot near the attacking blue line. A face-off also begins each period and is used as well after a goal and after any stoppage of play.

The goalie rarely leaves his goal area. The usual alignments of the other five players are three forwards—the centre, a left wing, and a right wing—and two defensemen—a left defenseman and a right defenseman.

A player may handle the puck as often or as long as he likes, so long as he does not close his glove on the puck or touch the puck with a stick that is higher than shoulder level. A player may not pass the puck with his open hand. The goalie, however, is generally not subject to these restrictions.

The game is divided into three periods of 20 minutes playing time each, with a 15-minute intermission between periods. Hockey games may end in a tie unless the rules stipulate an overtime period to serve as a tiebreaker. In the case of a tie in college hockey, one 10-minute sudden-death overtime period is played in regular season play. NHL teams play a five-minute sudden-death overtime period, followed by a shoot-out if the game remains tied. During the play-offs, college hockey has 10-minute overtime periods until there is a winner, while the NHL has the same system with 20-minute periods. There is generally no overtime period in international hockey; however, Olympic competition since 1994 has had a 10-minute sudden-death period, followed by a shootout if needed.

In organized ice hockey a victory is worth two points in the standings. A tie is worth one point, and the NHL, which has no ties, awards a point to a team that loses in overtime. A goal counts as a point for the team, but individual points may be awarded to as many as three players for one goal. One point goes to the player who scored the goal, and a point is awarded for an assist to each of the last two of the scorer's teammates who touched the puck, providing that the opposition did not handle the puck in the interim.

Ice hockey is the only major sport in which substitutions are permitted while the game is in play. The game is so fast and so demanding that forwards generally skate only 90 seconds at a time. Defensemen usually stay on the ice for a slightly longer period of time.

Because of the speed and contact, there are many infractions, not all of them having to do with "hitting" penalties. Play is stopped for an offside and for the infraction called icing, which occurs when a team shoots the puck out of its zone past the other team's goal line. Icing is not called against a team when it is shorthanded; if the teams are evenhanded or if the offending team has more players than the opposing team, the puck is returned to the defensive zone of the team that iced it for the face-off. No player, however, may delay the game by intentionally shooting the puck out of the rink or by shifting the goalposts.

Minor penalties are most commonly assessed for excessive use of the body or equipment to impede the opposition. For a minor infraction the offending player must remain in the penalty box at the side of the rink for two minutes while his team plays shorthanded. This man-advantage situation is called a power play. If the opponents score at any time during the penalty period, the penalized player may return to the ice. Penalties incurred by the goalie are served by a teammate. A major penalty for violent play results in the loss of a player for five minutes or for the remainder of the game. If major penalties are incurred simultaneously by both teams, substitutions are made and there is no shorthanded play. A game misconduct penalty for abusing an official results in the loss of a player for 10 minutes; however, a substitution is allowed, and the team does not play shorthanded.

There are three common types of shots in hockey: the slap shot, the wrist shot, and the backhander. The slap shot has been timed at more than 100 miles an hour (160 km an hour). The slap shot differs from the wrist shot in that the player brings his stick back until it is nearly perpendicular with the ice and then brings the stick down in an arc, swatting the puck as he follows through. It is not as accurate as the wrist shot, in which the player puts his stick on the ice near the puck and without a windup snaps his wrist to fire off a shot. The backhander is taken when the puck goes to the other side of the stick from which the player normally shoots. If he is a right-handed shooter, for example, he takes the backhander from his left side. It is taken when there is not enough time to shift the puck to his normal shooting position. The backhander generally is not as hard or as accurate as the wrist shot, but it has the advantage of being taken quickly.

Strategies

Speed is an essential requirement of the game. In the sport's early days a team could get away with having a few slow defensemen. But contests at all levels became so quick that offensive and defensive roles often are reversed, and defensemen may find themselves at the forefront of the action. Slower players must have other attributes to make a team; they must, for example, be able to check well, to prevent the other players from getting past them. But, since everyone on the team handles the puck at some point during a game, a premium is placed on puck-carrying ability. The man with the puck is in control, and the play can go only so fast as he directs it. Centre Wayne Gretzky, while playing for the Edmonton Oilers, was the dominant scorer in the NHL for most of the 1980s due to his outstanding puck handling and his accurate shooting and passing.

If a forward has the puck, the defensemen trail the play. If a defenseman is leading an offensive thrust, called a "rush," one of the forwards backs him up. The opposition, meanwhile, attempts to gain control of the puck or to dislodge it. The most common way is for the defending player to poke his stick at the puck. A defender may also block, check, or hit the player with his body, as long as his action falls within the rules defining allowable contact. Ideally, the defending team's defensemen lay back, straddling their blue line, away from the boards. They then can move to the centre to halt a breakthrough or can drive a man into the boards if he attempts to go along the sides. If the attacking players find that they have difficulty in stickhandling past the opposition, they may try a long shot "on goal." They may also shoot the puck into the other team's zone and chase it, two attacking players going after the puck—one to handle the opponent, who is sure to go after it, and the other to try to wrest the puck away. The third forward, meanwhile, takes up a position about 20 feet in front of the goal, in the centre of the ice, in a spot known as the "slot." In the slot he is in position to shoot if he gets the puck. The defensemen on the attacking team take up positions on the blue line to prevent the defending team from getting a breakaway. Often the puck is passed to the defensemen, who shoot from the blue line, 60 feet out, from their position known as the "point." Long shots rarely go in, so defensemen try to keep long shots low, which gives the attackers a chance at a rebound.

Many fans do not see goals scored in hockey because so many go in on rebounds or deflections. While a shot is taken, no attacking player may be in the goalie's crease, a rectangle eight feet across and four feet out from the goal line; but there is much physical contact in front of the net, and the puck may ricochet off a skate, a stick, or any part of the body. Any kind of shot that puts in a goal is allowable, unless the shooter has raised his stick above his elbow; but the puck may not be deliberately kicked in, and it cannot be thrown in with the hand.

One of the most unusual spectacles in hockey occurs when a team that is trailing by one goal takes its goaltender out of the net in the final seconds of the game. The goalie is replaced by a forward in the hope that the extra man on offense will give the team a chance for a tie, but this strategy sometimes results in the team without the extra man easily scoring what is called an "empty-net goal." Another rare and exciting play is the penalty shot, which is called when a stick is thrown to deflect a shot or when a player with an open path to the goal is pulled down from behind. The team against which the infraction was committed selects a player to skate unopposed to the opponent's goal and take one shot to beat the goalie; this generally results in a score for the shooting team.

NINE
TENNIS

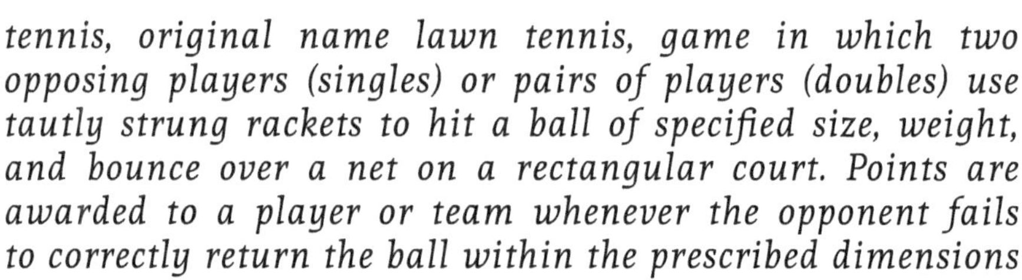

tennis, original name lawn tennis, game in which two opposing players (singles) or pairs of players (doubles) use tautly strung rackets to hit a ball of specified size, weight, and bounce over a net on a rectangular court. Points are awarded to a player or team whenever the opponent fails to correctly return the ball within the prescribed dimensions of the court. Organized tennis is played according to rules sanctioned by the International Tennis Federation (ITF), the world governing body of the sport.

Tennis originally was known as lawn tennis, and formally still is in Britain, because it was played on grass courts by Victorian gentlemen and ladies. It is now played on a variety of surfaces. The origins of the game can be traced to a 12th–13th-century French handball game called jeu de paume ("game of the palm"), from which was derived a complex indoor racket-and-ball game: real tennis. This ancient game is still played to a limited degree and is usually called real tennis in Britain, court tennis in the United States, and royal tennis in Australia.

Roger Federer

The modern game of tennis is played by millions in clubs and on public courts. Its period of most rapid growth as both a participant and a spectator sport began in the late 1960s, when the major championships were opened to professionals as well as amateurs, and continued in the 1970s, when television broadcasts of the expanding professional tournament circuits and the rise of some notable players and rivalries broadened the appeal of the game. A number of major innovations in fashion and equipment fueled and fed the boom. The addition of colour and style to tennis wear (once restricted to white) created an entirely new subdivision of leisure clothing. Tennis balls, which historically had been white, now came in several hues, with yellow the colour of choice. Racket frames, which had been of a standard size and shape and constructed primarily of laminated wood, were suddenly manufactured in a wide choice of sizes, shapes, and materials, the most significant milestones being the introduction of metal frames beginning in 1967 and the oversized head in 1976.

While tennis can be enjoyed by players of practically any level of skill, top competition is a demanding test of both shot making and stamina, rich in stylistic and strategic variety. From its origins as a garden-party game for ladies in whalebone corsets and starched petticoats and men in long white flannels, it has evolved into a physical chess match in which players attack and defend, exploiting angles and technical weaknesses with strokes of widely diverse pace and spin. Tournaments offer tens of millions of dollars in prize money annually.

BRITANNICA QUIZ

I Am the Greatest (Athlete)

The greatest of all time. Top of their sports. How well do you know them?

History

Origin and early years

There has been much dispute over the invention of modern tennis, but the officially recognized centennial of the game in 1973 commemorated its introduction by Major Walter Clopton Wingfield in 1873. He published the first book of rules that year and took out a patent on his game in 1874, although historians have concluded that similar games were played earlier and that the first tennis club was established by the Englishman Harry Gem and several associates in Leamington in 1872. Wingfield's court was of the hourglass shape and may have developed from badminton. The hourglass shape, stipulated by Wingfield in his booklet "Sphairistiké, or Lawn Tennis," may have been adopted for patent reasons since it distinguished the court from ordinary rectangular courts. At the time, the Marylebone Cricket Club (MCC) was the governing body of real tennis, whose rules it had recently revised. After J.M. Heathcote, a distinguished real tennis player, developed a better tennis ball of rubber covered with white flannel, the MCC in 1875 established a new, standardized set of rules for tennis.

Meanwhile, the game had spread to the United States in the 1870s. Mary Outerbridge of New York has been credited with bringing a set of rackets and balls to her brother, a director of the Staten Island Cricket and Baseball Club. But research has shown that William Appleton of Nahant, Massachusetts, may have owned the first lawn tennis set and that his friends James Dwight and Fred R. Sears popularized the game.

Get a Britannica Premium subscription and gain access to exclusive content.Subscribe Now

An important milestone in the history of tennis was the decision of the All England Croquet Club to set aside one of its lawns at Wimbledon for tennis, which soon proved so popular that the club changed its name to the All England Croquet and Lawn Tennis Club. In 1877 the club decided to hold a tennis championship, and a championship subcommittee of three was appointed. It decided on a rectangular court 78 feet (23.8 metres) long by 27 feet (8.2 metres) wide. They adapted the real tennis method of scoring—15, 30, 40, game—and allowed the server one fault (i.e., two chances to deliver a proper service on each point). These major decisions remain part of the modern rules. Twenty-two entries were received, and the first winner of the Wimbledon Championships was Spencer Gore. In 1878 the Scottish Championships were held, followed in 1879 by the Irish Championships.

There were several alterations in some of the other rules (e.g., governing the height of the net) until 1880, when the All England Club and the MCC published revised rules that approximate very closely those still in use. The All England Club was the dominant authority then, the British Lawn Tennis Association (LTA) not being formed until 1888. In 1880 the first U.S. championship was held at the Staten Island Cricket and Baseball Club. The victor was an Englishman, O.E. Woodhouse. The popularity of the game in the United States and frequent doubts about the rules led to the foundation in 1881 of the U.S. National Lawn Tennis Association, later renamed the U.S. Lawn Tennis Association and, in 1975, the U.S. Tennis Association (USTA). Under its auspices, the first official U.S. national championship, played under English rules, was held in 1881 at the Newport Casino, Newport, Rhode Island. The winner, Richard Sears, was U.S. champion for seven consecutive years.

Tennis had taken firm root in Australia by 1880, and the first Australian Championships were played in 1905. The first national championships in New Zealand were held in 1886. In 1904 the Lawn Tennis Association of Australasia (later of Australia) was founded.

The first French Championships were held at the Stade Français in 1891, but it was an interclub tournament that did not become truly international until 1925; the French Federation of Lawn Tennis was established in 1920. Other national championships were inaugurated in Canada (1890), South Africa (1891), Spain (1910), Denmark (1921), Egypt (1925), Italy (1930), and Sweden (1936). In 1884 a women's championship was introduced at Wimbledon, and women's national championships were held in the United States starting in 1887.

Outstanding players

Tennis in the 1880s was dominated by the remarkable twin brothers William and Ernest Renshaw. William won the Wimbledon singles championship seven times, on three occasions defeating his brother in the final. Ernest was victorious once, and in partnership they won the doubles championship, first played at Oxford in 1879, seven times.

In the 1890s public interest began to wane. The Wimbledon Championships showed a financial loss in 1894 and 1895; the All England Club committee turned back to croquet to revive its flagging fortunes. The popularity of Wimbledon and tennis were reestablished by two more brothers: Reginald and Laurie Doherty. Reginald won the Wimbledon singles from 1897 to 1900. Laurie won from 1902 to 1906, took the U.S. championship in 1903, and won a gold medal in the Olympic Games in 1900.

The first international team competition was the Davis Cup, officially called the International Lawn Tennis Challenge Trophy, which was donated by U.S. doubles champion Dwight Davis in 1900. Only Great Britain challenged the first year; it was defeated by the United States, Davis himself playing on the victorious team. There was no challenge in 1901, but in 1902 a strong British team that included the Doherty brothers went to America. The United States retained the trophy, but the following year the Doherty brothers helped Britain win the cup, which it retained the next three years.

The Doherty reign ended in 1906, but tennis was by then firmly established. The new star was Norman Brookes, the first in a long line of Australian champions and the first left-hander to reach the top. He won at Wimbledon in 1907 and again on his next visit, in 1914. He and his doubles partner, Tony Wilding of New Zealand, wrested the Davis Cup from Great Britain in 1907 and held it until 1911, arousing enduring public interest in Australia and New Zealand.

Of the women champions of the early 1900s, Dorothea Douglass (later Mrs. Lambert Chambers) won at Wimbledon seven times, beginning in 1903. In 1905, however, Douglass met her match in the first U.S. women's champion to win at Wimbledon, May Sutton, who again defeated her at

Wimbledon in 1907. The outbreak of World War I in 1914 interrupted tennis activities in Britain and Europe, but, with the exception of 1917, when a Patriotic Tournament was held, U.S. championships continued to be played.

The dominant champions of the early postwar years were Bill Tilden of the United States and Suzanne Lenglen of France. Tilden, the U.S. champion from 1920 through 1925 and again in 1929, won the Wimbledon title in 1920, 1921, and 1930. In the same period he also won 15 Davis Cup singles. Suzanne Lenglen reigned supreme over the ladies' game from 1919 to 1925; were it not for the war, she might have started her international career earlier. She won the Wimbledon championship at her first attempt in 1919, from 1920 to 1923, and in 1925, not competing in 1924 because of illness. She developed a powerful as well as accurate game by practicing with men, and she needed far more freedom of movement than restrictive ladies' fashion of that time allowed. Her first appearance at Wimbledon in a calf-length white dress with short sleeves and without petticoat or suspender (garter) belt caused a sensation.

France also made its mark on men's tennis with the fabulous "Four Musketeers"—Jean Borotra, Henri Cochet, René Lacoste, and Jacques Brugnon. Among them, they monopolized the Wimbledon singles title from 1924 through 1929, won 10 French and 3 U.S. singles championships, and won 5 Wimbledon and 10 French doubles championships. They captured the Davis Cup from the United States in 1927 and held it until 1933.

A new female American star, Helen Wills (later Mrs. Moody and then Mrs. Roark), won the first of her seven U.S. singles titles in 1923; she went on to win at Wimbledon eight times between 1927 and 1938 and won the French singles four times *between 1928 and 1932. (Wills wrote the article on lawn tennis for the 14th edition [1929] of the Encyclopædia Britannica.) Only once, early in her career, did she play against Lenglen, at Cannes on the French Riviera, where she lost in two straight sets. That historic meeting between the poker-faced Wills, in her trademark white eyeshade, and the flamboyant Lenglen, in her daring dress and silk bandeau, was chronicled in sports and society pages on both sides of the Atlantic. Wills's great rival, however, was another American, Helen Jacobs, Wimbledon champion in Wills's absence in 1936 and U.S. champion from 1932 to 1935.*

The Englishman Fred Perry won the Wimbledon singles for three consecutive years (1934–36), the U.S. championship in 1933, 1934, and 1936, the Australian in 1934, and the French in 1935. From the United States came champions that included Sidney Wood, Ellsworth Vines, and Don Budge, who in 1938 became the first man to win all four major titles—the Australian, French, Wimbledon, and U.S.—in one season, a feat that came to be known as the Grand Slam. Alice Marble, the most aggressive net rusher the women's game had seen to that time, won the U.S. singles in 1936 and from 1938 to 1940, and in 1939 she won the singles, doubles, and mixed doubles at Wimbledon, a "triple" previously accomplished only by Lenglen and Budge.

The development of the game was interrupted by World War II, but international tennis resumed in 1946 with American players again dominant, led by Jack Kramer, the U.S. champion of 1946–47 and Wimbledon champion of 1947 before he turned professional. He was succeeded by Pancho Gonzales, Bob Falkenburg, Frederick (Ted) Schroeder, J. Edward ("Budge") Patty, and Dick Savitt. American women won every Wimbledon and U.S. singles title from 1946 through 1958, the string of champions including Pauline Betz, Louise Brough, Margaret Osborne DuPont, Doris Hart,

Maureen Connolly, Shirley Fry, and Althea Gibson, the first black champion. Connolly, nicknamed "Little Mo," won the three Wimbledon and three U.S. championships that she played between 1951 and 1954 and in 1953 became the first woman to achieve the Grand Slam.

Australia ruled men's tennis in the 1950s and '60s, winning the Davis Cup in 15 of 18 years. Among the Wimbledon and U.S. singles champions who played for Harry Hopman, the outstanding nonplaying Australian captain, were Frank Sedgman, Lew Hoad, Ken Rosewall, Mal Anderson, Ashley Cooper, Neale Fraser, Rod Laver, Fred Stolle, Roy Emerson, and John Newcombe.

The broadening international horizons of the game were reflected in the Wimbledon triumphs of players such as Jaroslav Drobny, an expatriate Czech, in 1954 and Alex Olmedo, from Peru, in 1959 and in the victories of Mexican Rafael Osuna in the U.S. championship in 1963, Manuel Santana of Spain in the U.S. championship in 1965 and Wimbledon in 1966, and Brazilian Maria Bueno, the U.S. champion four times and Wimbledon champion three times between 1959 and 1966.

Australian Margaret Smith Court was the second woman to win the Grand Slam, in 1970, and she set the all-time record for singles, doubles, and mixed doubles titles in the four major championships: 65 between 1960 and 1975, including 3 Wimbledon, 6 U.S., 5 French, and 11 Australian singles. Billie Jean Moffitt King set a record for career Wimbledon titles, winning 6 singles, 10 doubles, and 4 mixed between 1961 and 1979.

The ITF and the national associations that constitute it govern tennis worldwide; they oversee international competitions such as the Davis Cup and Federation Cup and tennis in the Olympic Games, which was restored to medal-sport status for the 1988 Games—the first time since 1924. The professional circuits were governed from the late 1970s by the Men's and Women's International Professional Tennis councils. These groups, made up of representatives of the ITF, players, and tournaments, oversee the international calendar, the implementation of rules and codes of conduct, and the training and supervision of tour officials. The councils work closely with the ATP and WITA, which supply a number of services and benefits to players and tournaments and maintain rankings that provide the basis for entry into tournaments and seedings.

Until 1974, when South Africa won by default over India, only four nations had won the Davis Cup: Australia, Great Britain, France, and the United States. The championships of those four countries are the traditional "major" tournaments that make up the Grand Slam. Wimbledon in Britain is the oldest, having been played on the lawns of the All England Club since 1877. The French championships, played at Stade Roland-Garros in Auteuil, on the outskirts of Paris, are recognized as the world's premier clay-court tournaments. The U.S. championships were played on grass from their inception in 1881 through 1974; the next three years they were played on a synthetic clay surface at the West Side Tennis Club in Forest Hills, New York, and in 1978 the tournament moved to the rubberized asphalt courts of the USTA National Tennis Center in nearby Flushing Meadow Park. The Australian Championships were played on grass in several cities until 1968, when they moved to Melbourne; in 1988 they moved within that city to the synthetic courts of the new Australian National Tennis Centre.

The principal team events are the Davis Cup, Federation Cup, and Wightman Cup (U.S. versus British women). The Davis Cup series consists of five matches played over three days: two singles, one doubles, then two "reverse" singles. The Davis Cup draw was played in two zones from 1923 through 1965 and in four zones from 1966 through 1980. Starting in 1981, the top 16 teams competed in a World Group and all other participating nations in four zones. The Federation Cup, inaugurated in 1963, is contested at one site over a one-week period, each series consisting of three matches: two singles and a doubles. The Wightman Cup alternates between U.S. and British sites and consists of best-of-seven matches: five singles and two doubles.

TEN

WRESTLING

Wrestling, sport practiced in various styles by two competitors, involving forcing an opponent to touch the ground with some part of the body other than his feet; forcing him into a certain position, usually supine (on his back); or holding him in that position for a minimum length of time. Wrestling is conducted in various styles with contestants upright or on the ground (or mat).

The three basic types of wrestling contest are the belt-and-jacket, catch-hold, and loose styles, all of which appear to have originated in antiquity. Belt-and-jacket styles of wrestling are those in which the clothing of the wrestlers provides the principal means of taking a grip on the opponent. In many cases this is no more than a special belt worn by both wrestlers, while in others a special belted jacket and special trousers are worn. Catch-hold styles require the contestants to take a prescribed hold before the contest begins; often this grip must be maintained throughout the struggle. Loose styles of wrestling, which are used in modern international competition, commence with the wrestlers separated and free to seize any grip that they choose except such as are explicitly forbidden (e.g., taking hold of an opponent's clothing or using a life-threatening grip, such as a stranglehold).

Wrestling can also be classified in terms of what is required to win. These categories can be graded on an ascending scale of violence as follows: break-stance sports are those that require forcing the opponent to relinquish a certain posture or position; toppling requires that the standing opponent be forced to touch the ground with some part of his body other than his feet; touch-fall wrestling requires that the opponent be forced into a certain position, usually supine, for a brief instant; pin-fall wrestling requires that the opponent be held in such a position for a measurable length of time; and submission wrestling requires the opponent to vocally or visually signal defeat by his own choice.

Early history

No sport is older or more widely distributed than wrestling, often in highly local styles that have persisted to the present day.

Wrestling probably originated in hand-to-hand combat, and in particular as a sportive form of combat substituting the submission of a contestant for his death. Works of art from 3000 BCE depict belt wrestling in Babylonia and Egypt, and the Sumerian Gilgamesh epic has a description of such wrestling. Loose wrestling in India dates to before 1500 BCE. Chinese documents from 700 BCE describe loose wrestling, as do Japanese records from the 1ˢᵗ century BCE. The belt wrestling practiced locally in the 20ᵗʰ century by the Swiss, Icelanders, Japanese, and Cossacks differed little from that of the Egyptians in 2500 BCE.

Wrestling was probably the most popular sport of the ancient Greeks. Young men belonged to palaestras, or wrestling schools, as the focal point of their social life. Illustrations of wrestling on Greek vases and coins are common throughout all periods of ancient Greece, but all that can be told from it is that the style was loose wrestling and that wrestlers, as did all Greek athletes, competed naked. Wrestling was part of the Olympic Games from 776 BCE. There were two wrestling championships in these games: a toppling event for the best two of three falls; and the pankration (Latin: pancratium), which combined wrestling and boxing and ended in the submission of one contestant. Upright wrestling was also a part of the pentathlon event in the Olympic Games, a bout being fought to a clear-cut fall of one of the wrestlers. The most famous ancient Greek wrestler was Milon of Croton, who won the wrestling championship of the Olympic Games six times. Wrestling was less popular among the Romans than it had been with the Greeks, and, with the fall of the Roman Empire, references to wrestling disappeared in Europe until about 800 CE.

When the Islamic rulers of Persia began hiring Turkic mercenaries about 800 CE, the soldiers brought with them a style of loose wrestling called koresh, in which grips may be taken on the long, tight leather pants worn by the wrestlers and the bout ends with a touch fall of the loser briefly on his back. Gradually the Turks took over the entire Muslim dominion, and their wrestling style spread. Later Mongolian invasions in the 13th century introduced Mongolian wrestling, which received royal patronage, and wrestling became the national sport of modern Iran.

sumo wrestlers

Sumo, a Japanese belt-wrestling style, was a popular spectator sport under imperial patronage (710–1185). Originally a submission spectacle, sumo became highly ritualized as a toppling match with victory coming also from the forcing of an opponent out of a 12-foot (4-metre) circle. By the 17th century sumo wrestling had become a professional sport in Japan. From the samurai martial art jujitsu, judo, the other prominent Japanese wrestling style, was derived in the 19th century and became an international sport in the second half of the 20th century.

Wrestling occurred in several styles throughout Europe in the Middle Ages. The first recorded English match was held in London early in the 13th century. In England and Brittany a form of jacket wrestling commonly called Cornwall and Devon (see Cornish wrestling) survives from at least the 4th or 5th century. Wrestling as a martial skill was taught to the knights of the Holy Roman Empire, and wrestling instruction books appeared in manuscript before the introduction of printing and thereafter in print. Mongolian loose wrestling, introduced to India after the Mughal conquest of 1526, has survived in both India and Pakistan. As the modern era began, the English kings Henry VIII and Charles II and the French king Francis I were notable patrons of wrestling.

From the 18th century on, a procession of wrestlers or strongmen appeared at fairs, in theatres, and in circuses, challenging all comers, beginning with the Englishman Thomas Topham of London in the 18th century and culminating with Eugene Sandow, the German-born international figure, who continued into the 20th century. Early in the 1800s wrestling became a part of the training regimen of the German turnverein gymnastic movement. In the United States, wrestling was popular as a frontier sport (Abraham Lincoln was a noted local wrestler), bouts usually going until one contestant submitted and with few holds barred.

In the second half of the 19th century, two wrestling styles developed that ultimately dominated international wrestling: Greco-Roman wrestling and catch-as-catch-can, or freestyle wrestling. Greco-Roman wrestling, popularized first in France, was so called because it was thought to be the kind of wrestling done by the ancients. Greco-Roman wrestling involves holds made only above the waist and forbids wrapping the legs about an opponent when the wrestlers go down. Originally it was professional and popularized at international expositions held at Paris, but after its inclusion in the revived Olympic Games in 1896, Greco-Roman wrestling events were held at subsequent Olympic Games except in 1900 and 1904.

The second style, catch-as-catch-can, was popularized mainly in Great Britain and the United States, first as a professional sport and after 1888, when it was recognized by the Amateur Athletic Association, as an amateur sport. It was introduced into the Olympic Games of 1904 and contested thereafter except in 1912. Catch-as-catch-can permits holds above the waist and leg grips and is won by a pin-fall.

Freestyle, or international freestyle, wrestling is a synthetic form of catch-as-catch-can that came to be used in the Olympic Games after it first appeared in Antwerp about 1920. International freestyle is loose wrestling that uses the Greco-Roman touch-fall instead of the pin-fall common to Anglo-American wrestling practice.

Notable professional wrestlers in the late 19th and early 20th centuries included the Russian George Hackenschmidt, originally an amateur Greco-Roman wrestler who turned *professional and wrestled catch-as-catch-can from 1900. He was world champion until 1908. The American wrestler Frank Gotch defeated Hackenschmidt in 1908 and again in 1911.*

After Gotch's retirement in 1913, professional wrestling, which was already fighting a losing battle in popularity with boxing, came to an end as a serious professional sport. Thereafter, though its audience grew, especially in the United States, through radio broadcasts and later even more so through telecasts, it became pure spectacle. The winners, divided deliberately into "heroes" and "villains," were determined by promoters' financial requirements, not skill. Wrestling maneuvers became increasingly extravagant and artificial and lost most of their authenticity. Perhaps most theatrical of all is the style of professional wrestling known as lucha libre, a form that is commonly associated with Mexico and is known for its colourfully masked performers and aerial moves.

Though professional wrestling steadily declined in seriousness in the 20th century, significant improvements occurred in amateur wrestling during the same period. Originally there were no weight divisions in wrestling (the only weight in the first Olympic Games was heavyweight), but weight divisions developed in amateur wrestling. (For weight classes, see freestyle wrestling.) Earlier wrestling had been continuous and contested to one or two of three falls, sometimes with a time limit, sometimes without. Amateur wrestling came to be limited to three three-minute rounds effective in all international competition from 1967.

Perhaps most importantly, a system was devised in amateur wrestling to award points, short of a fall, based on one wrestler's being in control of another, so that draw matches were made virtually impossible. This system arose because Greco-Roman wrestling, with its restriction to holds only above the waist and the forbidden use of legs for holds, tended to be dull once the wrestlers were on the mat. In the 1912 Olympic Games two Finnish Greco-Roman wrestlers had a six-hour bout to no decision. In response to this problem, several American colleges introduced the idea of recording the length of time each wrestler was in control of the contest during the course of a bout. (A wrestler is in control when he is applying maneuvers that will eventuate in a pin-fall if his opponent is unable to escape.) In 1928 the National Collegiate Athletic Association adopted the collegiate style of wrestling as a national sport, and this resulted in the formulation of a set of point awards to keep a running score during a bout. The rules and judging are similar to those used in international freestyle and Greco-Roman bouts and include awarding points based on reversing control, applying a pinning hold, and placing an opponent in danger of pinning. The running point score and the difference in control time are used to decide a victor in no-fall bouts. The collegiate style of wrestling became increasingly popular in the high schools and colleges of the United States after World War II.

In the 20th century a third international style of wrestling, sambo, a kind of jacket wrestling, was created by Anatoly Kharlampiev of the Soviet Union and others after a study of various traditional wrestling styles. Sambo became popular in the Soviet Union, Bulgaria, and Japan and in 1964 was internationally recognized. In sambo a wrestler wins by throwing another cleanly on his back, or if the wrestlers go to the mat, the bout ends with the submission of one opponent. Sambo is much like judo and Mongolian wrestling, and bouts are of three three-minute rounds. There was never any attempt to organize professional wrestling in the Western world. Amateur organization was local and national from the early 19th century on, regional competition began *late in the 19th century, and in 1911 the Fédération Internationale de Lutte Amateur (FILA; International Amateur Wrestling Federation) was formed (reconstituted in 1920). The FILA regulates international competition, including the Olympic Games, and has held world championships in Greco-Roman wrestling from 1950 and in freestyle from 1951. World championships and Olympic championships in judo, sponsored by the International Judo Federation (formed in 1951), have been held from 1956 and 1964, respectively*

ELEVEN

BOXING

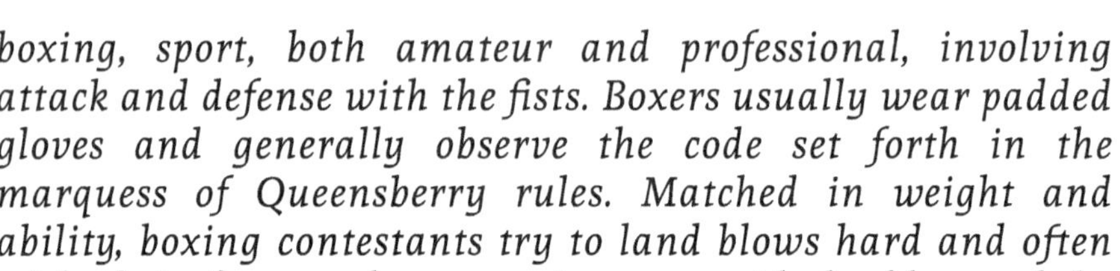

boxing, sport, both amateur and professional, involving attack and defense with the fists. Boxers usually wear padded gloves and generally observe the code set forth in the marquess of Queensberry rules. Matched in weight and ability, boxing contestants try to land blows hard and often with their fists, each attempting to avoid the blows of the opponent. A boxer wins a match either by outscoring the opponent—points can be tallied in several ways—or by rendering the opponent incapable of continuing the match. Bouts range from 3 to 12 rounds, each round normally lasting three minutes.

The terms pugilism and prizefighting in modern usage are practically synonymous with boxing, although the first term indicates the ancient origins of the sport in its derivation from the Latin pugil, "a boxer," related to the Latin pugnus, "fist," and derived in turn from the Greek pyx, "with clenched fist." The term prizefighting emphasizes pursuit of the sport for monetary gain, which began in England in the 17th century.

History

Early years

Boxing first appeared as a formal Olympic event in the 23rd Olympiad (688 BCE), but fist-fighting contests must certainly have had their origin in mankind's prehistory. The earliest visual evidence for boxing appears in Sumerian relief carvings from the 3rd millennium BCE. A relief sculpture from Egyptian Thebes (c. 1350 BCE) shows both boxers and spectators. The few extant Middle Eastern and Egyptian depictions are of bare-fisted contests with, at most, a simple band supporting the wrist; the earliest evidence of the use of gloves or hand coverings in boxing is a carved vase from Minoan Crete (c. 1500 BCE) that shows helmeted boxers wearing a stiff plate strapped to the fist.

The earliest evidence of rules for the sport comes from ancient Greece. These ancient contests had no rounds; they continued until one man either acknowledged defeat by holding up a finger or was unable to continue. Clinching (holding an opponent at close quarters with one or both arms) was strictly forbidden. Contests were held outdoors, which added the challenge of intense heat and bright sunlight to the fight. Contestants represented all social classes; in the early years of the major athletic festivals, a preponderance of the boxers came from wealthy and distinguished backgrounds.By the 4th century BCE, the simple ox-hide thongs described in the Iliad had been replaced by what the Greeks called "sharp thongs," which had a thick strip of hard leather over the knuckles that made them into lacerative weapons. Although the Greeks used padded gloves for practice, not dissimilar from the modern boxing glove, these gloves had no role in actual contests. The Romans developed a glove called the caestus (cestus) that is seen in Roman mosaics and described in their literature; this glove often had lumps of metal or spikes sewn into the leather. The caestus is an important feature in a boxing match in

Virgil's Aeneid (1ˢᵗ century BCE). The story of the match between Dares and Entellus is majestically told in this passage from the pugilism article in the 11ᵗʰ edition of Encyclopædia Britannica:

Boxing history picks up again with a formal bout recorded in Britain in 1681, and by 1698 regular pugilistic contests were being held in the Royal Theatre of London. The fighters performed for whatever purses were agreed upon plus stakes (side bets), and admirers of the combatants wagered on the outcomes. These matches were fought without gloves and, for the most part, without rules. There were no weight divisions; thus, there was just one champion, and lighter men were at an obvious disadvantage. Rounds were designated, but a bout was usually fought until one participant could no longer continue. Wrestling was permitted, and it was common to fall on a foe after throwing him to the ground. Until the mid 1700s it was also common to hit a man when he was down.

Although boxing was illegal, it became quite popular, and by 1719 the prizefighter James Figg had so captured the public's imagination that he was acclaimed champion of England, a distinction he held for some 15 years. One of Figg's pupils, Jack Broughton, is credited with taking the first steps toward boxing's acceptance as a respectable athletic endeavour. One of the greatest bare-knuckle prizefighters in history, Broughton devised the modern sport's first set of rules in 1743, and those rules, with only minor changes, governed boxing until they were replaced by the more detailed London Prize Ring rules in 1838. It is said that Broughton sought such regulations after one of his opponents died as a result of his fight-related injuries.

Broughton discarded the barroom techniques that his predecessors favoured and relied primarily on his fists. While wrestling holds were still permitted, a boxer could not grab an opponent below the waist. Under Broughton's rules, a round continued until a man went down; after 30 seconds he had to face his opponent (square off), standing no more than a yard (about a metre) away, or be declared beaten. Hitting a downed opponent was also forbidden. Recognized as the "Father of Boxing," Broughton attracted pupils to the sport by introducing "mufflers," the forerunners of modern gloves, to protect the fighter's hands and the opponent's face. (Ironically, these protective devices would prove in some ways to be more dangerous than bare fists. When boxers wear gloves, they are more likely to aim for their opponent's head, whereas, when fighters used their bare hands, they tended to aim for softer targets to avoid injuring the hand. Thus, the brain damage associated with boxing can be traced in part to the introduction of the padded boxing glove.)

After Jack Slack beat Broughton in 1750 to claim the championship, fixed fights (fights in which outcomes were predetermined) became common, and boxing again experienced a period of decline, though there were exceptions—pugilists Daniel Mendoza and Gentleman John Jackson were great fighters of the late 1700s. Mendoza weighed only 160 pounds (73 kg), and his fighting style therefore emphasized speed over brute strength. Jackson, who eventually defeated Mendoza to claim the championship, contributed to the transformation of boxing by interesting members of the English aristocracy in the sport, thus bringing it a degree of respectability. During the early to mid 1800s, some of the greatest British champions, including Jem Belcher, Tom Cribb, Ben Caunt, and Jem Mace, came to symbolize ideals of manliness and honour for the English.

After the British Pugilists' Protective Association initiated the London Prize Ring rules in 1838, the new regulations spread quickly throughout Britain and the United States. First used in a championship fight in 1839 in which James ("Deaf") Burke lost the English title to William Thompson ("Bendigo"), the new rules provided for a ring 24 feet (7.32 metres) square bounded by two ropes. When a fighter went down, the round ended, and he was helped to his corner. The next round would begin 30 seconds later, with each boxer required to reach, unaided, a mark in the centre of the ring. If a fighter could not reach that mark by the end of 8 additional seconds, he was declared the loser. Kicking, gouging, butting with the head, biting, and low blows were all declared fouls.

The era of Regency England was the peak of British boxing, when the champion of bare-knuckle boxing in Britain was considered to be the world champion as well. Britain's only potential rival in pugilism was the United States. Boxing had been introduced in the United States in the late 1700s but began to take root there only about 1800 and then only in large urban areas such as Boston, New York City, Philadelphia, and to some extent New Orleans. Most of the fighters who fought in the United States had emigrated from either England or Ireland; because boxing was then considered to be the national sport of Britain, there were few American-born fighters of the time.

Boxing's hold upon the British imagination is evidenced in the many idioms taken from pugilism that entered the English language during this period. Phrases such as come up to scratch (to meet the qualifications), start from scratch (to start over from the beginning), and not up to the mark (not up to the necessary level) all refer to the line that was scratched in the dirt to divide the ring. At the beginning of each round, both boxers were required to put their toes up against the line to prove they were fit enough for the bout. If they were unable to do so, they were said to be unable to come up to scratch, or to the mark. The term draw, meaning a tied score, derives from the stakes that held the rope surrounding the ring: when the match was over, the stakes were "drawn" out from the ground, and eventually the finality of taking down the ropes came to stand for the end of an inconclusive fight. Further, these stakes were also the basis behind the monetary meaning of stakes. In early prizefights a bag of money, which would go to the winner of the bout, was hung from one of the stakes—thus high stakes and stake money. As for the ropes held by the stakes, to be against the ropes connotes a posture of defense against an aggressive opponent. And any telling point in an argument is spoken of as being a knockout blow, and a beautiful woman as being a knockout.

The Queensberry rules

Though the London Prize Ring rules did much to help boxing, the brawling that distinguished old-time pugilism continued to alienate most of England's upper class, and it became apparent that still more revisions were necessary to attract a better class of patron. John Graham Chambers of the Amateur Athletic Club devised a new set of rules in 1867 that emphasized boxing technique and skill. Chambers sought the patronage of John Sholto Douglas, the 9th marquess of Queensberry, who lent his name to the new guidelines. The Queensberry rules differed from the London rules in four major respects: contestants wore padded gloves; a round consisted of three minutes of fighting followed by a minute of rest; wrestling was illegal; and any fighter who went down had to get up unaided within 10 seconds—if a fighter was unable to get up, he was declared knocked out, and the fight was over. During this period the introduction of the first weight divisions also took place.

The new rules at first were scorned by professionals, who considered them unmanly, and championship bouts continued to be fought under London Prize Ring rules. But many young pugilists preferred the Queensberry guidelines and fought accordingly. Prominent among these was James ("Jem") Mace, who won the English heavyweight title under the London rules in 1861. Mace's enthusiasm for gloved fighting did much to popularize the Queensberry rules.

In addition to the shift in rules, dominance in the ring began to slowly shift to American fighters. The change started, perhaps, with American fighters competing in Britain during the Regency era. Two such early fighters were former slaves—Bill Richmond and his protégé Tom Molineaux. Both Richmond and Molineaux fought against the top English pugilists of the day; indeed, Molineaux fought Tom Cribb twice for the championship title, in 1810 and 1811. Soon British champions began touring the United States and fighting American opponents.

Despite the change to the Queensberry rules, boxing was losing the social acceptability it had gained in England—partly because of changing middle-class values and an Evangelical religious revival intensely concerned about sinful pastimes. Boxing, after all, had close associations with such unsavoury practices as drinking and gambling. Further, the violence of boxing was not confined to the boxers—the spectators themselves, who often bet heavily on matches, were prone to crowd into the ring and fight as well. Large brawls frequently ensued.

Rule changes in British boxing took into account not only shifts in societal norms but the inescapable fact that the sport was illegal. The primary task of proponents was to reconcile a putatively barbaric activity with a civilizing impulse. According to English law, as reported in William Blackstone's Commentaries on the Laws of England (1765–69), "a tilt or tournament, the martial diversion of our ancestors is an unlawful act: and so are boxing and sword playing, the succeeding amusements of their posterity." Perceived by the courts as a throwback to a less-civilized past, prizefighting was classified as an affray, an assault, and a riot. However, widespread public support for boxing in England led to legal laxity and inconsistency of enforcement.

In the United States the response was different. There a combination of Puritan values and fears of lawlessness often produced heightened judicial vigilance. As the frequency of prizefights increased, various states moved beyond general and sometimes vague statutes concerning assault and enacted laws that expressly forbade fistfights. In 1876 the Massachusetts State Supreme Court confirmed its intention to maintain a lawful and ordered society by ruling that "prizefighting, boxing matches, and encounters of that kind serve no useful purpose, tend to breaches of the peace, and are unlawful even when entered into by agreement and without anger or ill will." Boxing thus took a course of evasion by bringing a greater appearance of order to the sport through changes in rules and by relocation to more lenient environments. Matches were frequently held in remote backwaters and were not openly publicized in order that the fighters might avoid arrest; barges were also used as fight venues because they could be located in waters outside U.S. legal jurisdiction and fights could be held unimpeded.

Eventually the ever-growing popularity and profitability of the sport combined with its hero-making potential forced a reconsideration of boxing's value by many state authorities. The fact that the heavyweight champion of boxing came to symbolize American might and resolve, even dominance, had a significant impact on the sport's acceptance. Likewise, its role as a training tool in World War I left many with the impression that boxing, if conducted under proper conditions, lent itself to the development of skill, courage, and character.

Thus, the very authorities who had fined and jailed pugilists came to sanction and regulate their activities through state boxing and athletic commissions. State regulation became the middle ground between outright prohibition and unfettered legalization.

TWELVE

BASKETBALL

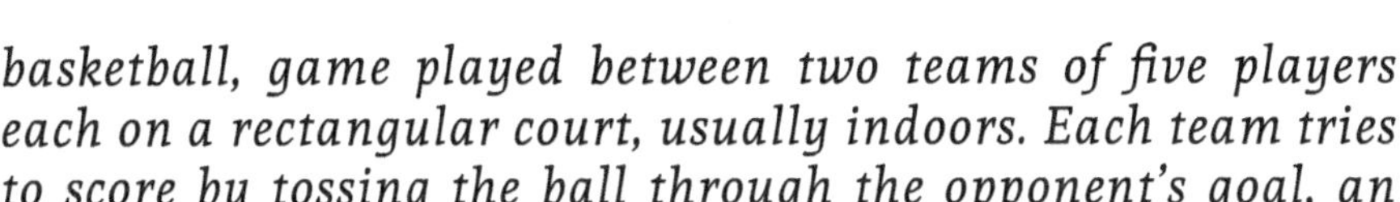

basketball, game played between two teams of five players each on a rectangular court, usually indoors. Each team tries to score by tossing the ball through the opponent's goal, an elevated horizontal hoop and net called a basket.

The only major sport strictly of U.S. origin, basketball was invented by James Naismith (1861–1939) on or about December 1, 1891, at the International Young Men's Christian Association (YMCA) Training School (now Springfield College), Springfield, Massachusetts, where Naismith was an instructor in physical education.

For that first game of basketball in 1891, Naismith used as goals two half-bushel peach baskets, which gave the sport its name. The students were enthusiastic. After much running and shooting, William R. Chase made a midcourt shot—the only score in that historic contest. Word spread about the newly invented game, and numerous associations wrote Naismith for a copy of the rules, which were published in the January 15, 1892, issue of the Triangle, the YMCA Training School's campus paper.

While basketball is competitively a winter sport, it is played on a 12-month basis—on summer playgrounds, in municipal, industrial, and church halls, in school yards and family driveways, and in summer camps—often on an informal basis between two or more contestants. Many grammar schools, youth groups, municipal recreation centres, churches, and other organizations conduct basketball programs for youngsters of less than high school age. Jay Archer, of Scranton, Pennsylvania, introduced "biddy" basketball in 1950 for boys and girls under 12 years of age, the court and equipment being adjusted for size.In the early years the number of players on a team varied according to the number in the class and the size of the playing area. In 1894 teams began to play with five on a side when the playing area was less than 1,800 square feet (167.2 square metres); the number rose to seven when the gymnasium measured from 1,800 to 3,600 square feet (334.5 square metres) and up to nine when the playing area exceeded that. In 1895 the number was occasionally set at five by mutual consent; the rules stipulated five players two years later, and this number has remained ever since.Since Naismith and five of his original players were Canadians, it is not surprising that Canada was the first country outside the United States to play the game. Basketball was introduced in France in 1893, in England in 1894, in Australia, China, and India soon thereafter, and in Japan in 1900.

While basketball helped swell the membership of YMCAs because of the availability of their gyms, within five years the game was outlawed by various associations because gyms that had been occupied by classes of 50 or 60 members were now monopolized by only 10 to 18 players. The banishment of the game induced many members to terminate their YMCA membership and to hire halls to play the game, thus paving the way to the professionalization of the sport.

Originally, players wore one of three styles of uniforms: knee-length football trousers; jersey tights, as commonly worn by wrestlers; or short padded pants, forerunners of today's uniforms, plus knee guards. The courts often were of irregular shape with occasional obstructions such as pillars, stairways, or offices that interfered with play. In 1903 it was ruled that all boundary lines must be straight. In 1893 the Narragansett Machinery Co. of Providence, Rhode Island, marketed a hoop of iron with a hammock style of basket. Originally a ladder, then a pole, and finally a chain fastened to the bottom of the net was used to retrieve a ball after a goal had been scored. Nets open at the bottom were adopted in 1912–13. In 1895–96 the points for making a basket (goal, or field goal) were reduced from three to two, and the points for making a free throw (shot uncontested from a line in front of the basket after a foul had been committed) were reduced from three to one.

Baskets were frequently attached to balconies, making it easy for spectators behind a basket to lean over the railings and deflect the ball to favour one side and hinder the other; in 1895 teams were urged to provide a 4-by-6-foot (1.2-by-1.8-metre) screen for the purpose of eliminating interference. Soon after, wooden backboards proved more suitable. Glass backboards were legalized by the professionals in 1908–09 and by colleges in 1909–10. In 1920–21 the backboards were moved 2 feet (0.6 metre), and in 1939–40 4 feet, in from the end lines to reduce frequent stepping out-of-bounds. Fan-shaped backboards were made legal in 1940–41.

A soccer ball (football) was used for the first two years. In 1894 the first basketball was marketed. It was laced, measured close to 32 inches (81 cm), or about 4 inches (10 cm) larger than the soccer ball, in circumference, and weighed less than 20 ounces (567 grams). By 1948–49, when the laceless molded ball was made official, the size had been set at 30 inches (76 cm).

The first college to play the game was either Geneva College (Beaver Falls, Pennsylvania) or the University of Iowa. C.O. Bemis heard about the new sport at Springfield and tried it out with his students at Geneva in 1892. At Iowa, H.F. Kallenberg, who had attended Springfield in 1890, wrote Naismith for a copy of the rules and also presented the game to his students. At Springfield, Kallenberg met Amos Alonzo Stagg, who became athletic director at the new University of Chicago in 1892. The first college basketball game with five on a side was played between the University of Chicago and the University of Iowa in Iowa City on January 18, 1896. The University of Chicago won, 15–12, with neither team using a substitute. Kallenberg refereed that game—a common practice in that era—and some of the spectators took exception to some of his decisions.

The colleges formed their own rules committee in 1905, and by 1913 there were at least five sets of rules: collegiate, YMCA–Amateur Athletic Union, those used by state militia groups, and two varieties of professional rules. Teams often agreed to play under a different set for each half of a game. To establish some measure of uniformity, the colleges, Amateur Athletic Union, and YMCA formed the Joint Rules Committee in 1915. This group was renamed the National Basketball Committee (NBC) of the United States and Canada in 1936 and until 1979 served as the game's sole amateur rule-making body. In that year, however, the colleges broke away to form their own rules committee, and during the same year the National Federation of State High School Associations likewise assumed the task of establishing separate playing rules for the high schools. The National Collegiate Athletic Association (NCAA) Rules Committee for men is a 12-member board representing all three NCAA divisions. It has six members from Division I schools and three each from

Divisions II and III. It has jurisdiction over colleges, junior colleges, the National Association of Intercollegiate Athletics (NAIA), and Armed Forces basketball. There is a similar body for women's play.

Growth of the game

Basketball grew steadily but slowly in popularity and importance in the United States and internationally in the first three decades after World War II. Interest in the game deepened as a result of television exposure, but with the advent of cable television, especially during the 1980s, the game's popularity exploded at all levels. Given a timely mix of spectacular players—such as Earvin ("Magic") Johnson, Julius Erving ("Dr. J"), Larry Bird, and Michael Jordan—and the greatly increased exposure, basketball moved quickly to the forefront of the American sporting scene, alongside such traditional leaders as baseball and football. Four areas of the game developed during this period: U.S. high school and college basketball, professional basketball, women's basketball, and international basketball.

U.S. high school and college basketball

Basketball at the high school and college levels developed from a structured, rigid game in the early days to one that is often fast-paced and high-scoring. Individual skills improved markedly, and, although basketball continued to be regarded as the ultimate team game, individualistic, one-on-one performers came to be not only accepted but used as an effective means of winning games.

In the early years games were frequently won with point totals of less than 30, and the game, from the spectator's viewpoint, was slow. Once a team acquired a modest lead, the popular tactic was to stall the game by passing the ball without trying to score, in an attempt to run out the clock. The NBC, seeing the need to discourage such slowdown tactics, instituted a number of rule changes. In 1932–33 a line was drawn at midcourt, and the offensive team was required to advance the ball past it within 10 seconds or lose possession. Five years later, in 1937–38, the centre jump following each field goal or free throw was eliminated. Instead, the defending team was permitted to inbound the ball from the out-of-bounds line underneath the basket. Decades passed before another alteration of like magnitude was made in the college game. After experimentation, the NCAA Rules Committee installed a 45-second shot clock in 1985 (reduced to 35 seconds in 1993), restricting the time a team could control the ball before shooting, and one year later it implemented a three-point shot rule for baskets made beyond a distance of 19.75 feet (6.0 metres). In 2008 the three-point line was moved to 20.75 feet (6.3 metres) from the basket.

More noticeable alteration in the game came at both the playing and coaching levels. Stanford University's Hank Luisetti was the first to use and popularize the one-hand shot in the late 1930s. Until then the only outside attempts were two-handed push shots. In the 1950s and '60s a shooting style evolved from Luisetti's push-off one hander to a jump shot, which is released at the top of the jump. West Virginia University guard Jerry West and Purdue University's Rick Mount were two players who demonstrated the devastating effectiveness of this shot.

Coaching strategy changed appreciably over the years. Frank W. Keaney, coach at the University of Rhode Island from

1921 to 1948, is credited with introducing the concept of "fast break" basketball, in which the offensive team rushes the ball upcourt hoping to get a good shot before the defense can get set. Another man who contributed to a quicker pace of play, particularly through the use of the pressure defense, was Adolph Rupp, who became the University of Kentucky's coach in 1931 and turned its program into one of the most storied in basketball history.

Defensive coaching philosophy, similarly, has undergone change. Whereas pioneer coaches such as Henry Iba of Oklahoma A&M University (now Oklahoma State University) or Long Island University's Clair Bee taught strictly a man-to-man defense, the zone defense, developed by Cam Henderson of Marshall University in West Virginia, later became an integral part of the game (see below Play of the game).

Over the years one of the rules makers' chief concerns was to neutralize the advantage of taller players. At 6 feet 5 inches (1.96 metres) Joe Lapchick was considered very tall when he played for the Original Celtics in the 1920s, but, as even taller players appeared, rules were changed in response. To prevent tall players from stationing themselves near the basket, a rule was instituted in 1932–33 prohibiting the player with the ball from standing inside the foul lane with his back to the basket for more than three seconds; the three-second rule later applied to any attacking player in the foul lane. In 1937–38 a new rule forbade any player from touching the ball when it was in the basket or on its rim (basket interference), and in 1944–45 it became illegal for any defending player to touch the ball on its downward flight toward the basket (goaltending).

Nevertheless, with each passing decade, the teams with the tallest players tended to dominate. Bob Kurland (7 feet [2.13 metres]) led Oklahoma A&M to two NCAA championships in the 1940s and led the nation in scoring in 1945–46. In the same era George Mikan (6 feet 10 inches [2.08 metres]) scored more than 550 points in each of his final two seasons at DePaul University before going on to play nine professional seasons in which he scored more than 11,000 points. Mikan was an outstanding player, not only because of his size but because of his ability to shoot sweeping hook shots with both hands.

In the 1950s Bill Russell (6 feet 9 inches [2.06 metres]) led the University of San Francisco to two NCAA championships before going on to become one of the greatest centres in professional basketball history. Wilt Chamberlain (7 feet 1 inch [2.16 metres]) played at the University of Kansas before turning professional in the late 1950s and is regarded as the greatest all-around big man ever to play. It remained, however, for Lew Alcindor (later Kareem Abdul-Jabbar), also 7 feet 1 inch, to most influence the rules. After his sophomore year (1966–67) at the University of California at Los Angeles (UCLA), the dunk shot was banned from collegiate basketball, ostensibly because the rules committee felt, again, that the big men had too great an advantage. The rule was rescinded beginning with the 1976–77 season, and the dunk shot became an important part of the game, electrifying both fans and players.

So too have the small- and medium-size players affected the game's development. Bob Cousy, playing at Holy Cross College and later for the Boston Celtics, was regarded as one of the game's first great playmakers. He was among the first to use the behind-the-back pass and between-the-legs dribble as effective offensive maneuvers. Later such smaller players as Providence College's Ernie DiGregorio, the University of

North Carolina's Phil Ford, and Indiana's Isiah Thomas proved the importance of their role. Between those two extremes are players such as Louisiana State University's Pete Maravich, who set an all-time collegiate scoring record of 44.5 points per game in the 1969–70 season; Magic Johnson, the point guard who led Michigan State University to a championship in 1979 and the Los Angeles Lakers to several NBA championships; Oscar Robertson, a dominating performer for the University of Cincinnati in the late 1950s and for the Milwaukee Bucks in the 1970s; Larry Bird of Indiana State University, a forward of exceptional versatility who led the Boston Celtics to several championships; and Michael Jordan, a great all-around player with the University of North Carolina in the 1980s who is widely considered the best professional player in the history of the sport.

Nothing influenced the college game's growth more than television, however. The NCAA championship games were televised nationally from 1963, and by the 1980s all three major television networks were telecasting intersectional college games during the November-to-March season. Rights fees for these games soared from a few million dollars to well over $50 million by the late 1980s. As for broadcasting the NCAA finals, a television contract that began in 2003 gave the NCAA an average of $545 million per year for the television rights; this exponential growth in broadcast fees reflected the importance of these games to both networks and advertisers.

www.ingramcontent.com/pod-product-compliance
Lightning Source LLC
Chambersburg PA
CBHW071328140726
47996CB00005B/1876